A CENTURY *of* BRISTOL

Queen Victoria lived just twenty-six days into the twentieth century: she died on 26 January 1901 and Albert Edward, the Prince of Wales, was declared King Edward VII. On 24 June 1902 the city's streets were decorated for the Coronation and here we see the headquarters of Sir George White, owner of the tramway company and the then new aircraft works at Filton, festooned in garlands of flowers, greenery, flags and bearing the monograms of the King and Queen Alexandra. Unfortunately, the King was ill and the Coronation had to be postponed until 9 August.

A CENTURY *of* BRISTOL

DAVID J. EVELEIGH

SUTTON PUBLISHING

First published in the United Kingdom in 1999 by
Sutton Publishing Limited · Phoenix Mill
Thrupp · Stroud · Gloucestershire · GL5 2BU

British Library Cataloguing in Publication Data
A catalogue record for this book is available from the British Library.

ISBN 0-7509-2426-8

Front endpaper: City Docks, late 1920s, showing the close physical relationship between the city centre and the City Docks. Changes, however, came soon: in the mid-1930s the construction of Temple Way and Redcliffe Way – the first sections of an inner circuit road – would cut a swathe through old properties in Redcliff and result in the construction of Redcliff Bridge and a new road cutting diagonally across Queens Square. German air raids then caused extensive damage around the docks: the large Corporation granary (centre) was destroyed in January 1941 and St Raphael's church and almshouses nearby badly damaged.
Back endpaper: A computer-simulated view of St Augustine's Reach showing the @ Bristol development on Canons Marsh, due to open in spring 2000. It contains two 'high-tech' attractions – Wildscreen @ Bristol, interpreting the natural world, and a science discovery centre – Explore @ Bristol. The scheme is at the heart of a major redevelopment of the waterside area at Canons Marsh and is being sponsored by the Millennium Commission, the South West Regional Development Agency and Bristol City Council with considerable private sector funding.
Half title page: A view of the centre from Baldwin Street, *c*. 1947.
Title page: Pim's Court, Horsefair, *c*. 1933. (See also page 65)

A clown juggles to an appreciative audience at Goram's Fair *c*. 1958.

Typeset in 11/14pt Photina.
Typesetting and origination by
Sutton Publishing Limited.
Printed in Great Britain by
The Bath Press, Bath.

Contents

BRITAIN: A CENTURY OF CHANGE
Roger Hudson 7

BRISTOL: AN INTRODUCTION 13

EDWARDIAN BRISTOL 19

THE FIRST WORLD WAR 33

BETWEEN THE WARS 43

THE SECOND WORLD WAR 65

THE POSTWAR PERIOD 73

THE 1960S AND '70S 91

MODERN BRISTOL 109

ACKNOWLEDGEMENTS AND PICTURE CREDITS 121

Fry's number 5 factory on the corner of Union Street and Broadmead, 1936. This imposing corner block of brick and granite, four storeys high, was built in the early 1890s when Frys were rapidly expanding their works. The ground floor contained a large showroom and the top floor was originally called the chapel floor but later used as a theatre and staff dancing room. In 1936, following the completion of Fry's transfer to Somerdale, the city centre factories were closed. Some of the buildings survived into the 1960s but this block was demolished in early 1937 to make way for the Odeon cinema. The tramlines sweep around the corner from Broadmead into Lower Union Street while the traffic lights controlling the junction were still a relatively new item of street furniture.

Britain: A Century of Change

Children gathered around an early wireless set in the 1920s. The speed and forms of communication were to change dramatically as the century advanced. (*Barnaby's Picture Library*)

The delirious rejoicing at the news of the Relief of Mafeking, during the Boer War in May 1900, is a colourful historical moment. But, in retrospect, the introduction that year of the first motor bus was rather more important, signalling another major adjustment to town life. In the previous 60 years railway stations, post-and-telegraph offices, police and fire stations, gas works and gasometers, new livestock markets and covered markets, schools, churches, football grounds, hospitals and asylums, water pumping stations and sewerage plants had totally altered the urban scene, as the country's population tripled and over 70 per cent were born in or moved to the towns.

When Queen Victoria died in 1901, she was measured for her coffin by her grandson Kaiser Wilhelm, the London prostitutes put on black mourning and the blinds came down in the villas and terraces spreading out from the old town centres. These centres were reachable by train and tram, by the new bicycles and still newer motor cars, connected by the new telephone, and lit by gas or even electricity. The shops may have been full of British-made cotton and woollen clothing but the grocers and butchers were selling cheap Danish bacon, Argentinian beef, Australasian mutton, tinned or dried fish and fruit from Canada, California and South Africa. Most of these goods were carried in British-built-and-crewed ships, burning Welsh steam coal.

Women working as porters on the Great Western Railway, Paddington, *c.* 1917. (*W.L. Kenning/Adrian Vaughan Collection*)

As the first decade moved on, the Open Spaces Act meant more parks, bowling greens and cricket pitches. The first state pensions came in, together with higher taxation and death duties. These were raised mostly to pay for the new Dreadnought battleships needed to maintain naval superiority over Germany, and deter them from war. But the deterrent did not work. The First World War transformed the place of women, as they took over many men's jobs. Its other legacies were the war memorials which joined the statues of Victorian worthies in main squares round the land. After 1918 death duties bit even harder and a quarter of England changed hands in a few years.

The multiple shop – the chain store – appeared in the high street: Sainsburys, Maypole, Lipton's, Home & Colonial, the Fifty Shilling Tailor, Burton, Boots, W.H. Smith. The shopper was spoilt for choice, attracted by the brash fascias and advertising hoardings for national brands like Bovril, Pears Soap, and Ovaltine. Many new buildings began to be seen, such as garages, motor showrooms, picture palaces (cinemas), 'palais de dance', and the bow-windowed, pebble-dashed, tile-hung, half-timbered houses that were built as ribbon-development along the roads and new bypasses or on the new estates nudging the green belts.

During the 1920s cars became more reliable and sophisticated as well as commonplace, with developments like the electric self-starter making them easier for women to drive. Who wanted to turn a crank handle in the new short skirt? This was, indeed, the electric age as much as the motor era. Trolley buses, electric trams and trains extended mass transport and electric light replaced gas in the street and the home, which itself was groomed by the vacuum cleaner.

Father and child cycling past Buckingham Palace on VE Day, 8 May 1945. (*Hulton Getty Picture Collection*)

A major jolt to the march onward and upward was administered by the Great Depression of the early 1930s. The older British industries – textiles, shipbuilding, iron, steel, coal – were already under pressure from foreign competition when this worldwide slump arrived, cutting exports by half in two years and producing 3 million unemployed (and still rising) by 1932. Luckily there were new diversions to alleviate the misery. The 'talkies' arrived in the cinemas; more and more radios and gramophones were to be found in people's homes; there were new women's magazines, with fashion, cookery tips and problem pages; football pools; the flying feats of women pilots like Amy Johnson; the Loch Ness Monster; cheap chocolate and the drama of Edward VIII's abdication.

Things were looking up again by 1936 and unemployment was down to 2 million. New light industry was booming in the Home Counties as factories struggled to keep up with the demand for radios, radiograms, cars and electronic goods including the first television sets. The threat from Hitler's Germany meant rearmament, particularly of the airforce, which stimulated aircraft and aero engine firms. If you were lucky and lived in the south, there was good money to be earned. A semi-detached house cost £450, a Morris Cowley £150. People may have smoked like chimneys but life expectancy, since 1918, was up by 15 years while the birth rate had almost halved. The fifty-four hour week was down to forty-eight hours and there were 9 million radio licences by 1939.

In some ways it is the little memories that seem to linger longest from the Second World War: the kerbs painted white to show up in the blackout, the rattle of ack-ack shrapnel on roof tiles, sparrows killed by bomb blast, painting your legs brown and then adding a black seam

A family gathered around their television set in the 1950s. (*Hulton Getty Picture Collection*)

down the back to simulate stockings. The biggest damage, apart from London, was in the south-west (Plymouth, Bristol) and the Midlands (Coventry, Birmingham). Postwar reconstruction was rooted in the Beveridge Report which set out the expectations for the Welfare State. This, together with the nationalisation of the Bank of England, coal, gas, electricity and the railways, formed the programme of the Labour government in 1945. At this time the USA was calling in its debts and Britain was beggared by the war, yet still administering its Empire.

Times were hard in the late 1940s, with rationing even more stringent than during the war. Yet this was, as has been said, 'an innocent and well-behaved era'. The first let-up came in 1951 with the Festival of Britain and then there was another fillip in 1953 from the Coronation, which incidentally gave a huge boost to the spread of TV. By 1954 leisure motoring had been resumed but the Comet – Britain's best hope for taking on the American aviation industry – suffered a series of mysterious crashes. The Suez debacle of 1956 was followed by an acceleration in the withdrawal from Empire, which had begun in 1947 with the Independence of India. Consumerism was truly born with the advent of commercial TV and most homes soon boasted washing machines, fridges, electric irons and fires.

The *Lady Chatterley* obscenity trial in 1960 was something of a straw in the wind for what was to follow in that decade. A collective loss of inhibition seemed to sweep the land, as stately home owners opened up, the Beatles and the Rolling Stones transformed popular music, and retailing, cinema and the theatre were revolutionised. Designers, hairdressers, photographers and models moved into places vacated by an Establishment put to flight by the new breed of satirists spawned by *Beyond the Fringe* and *Private Eye.*

In the 1970s Britain seems to have suffered a prolonged hangover after the excesses of the previous decade. Ulster, inflation and union troubles were not made up for by entry into the EEC, North Sea Oil, Women's Lib or, indeed, Punk Rock. Mrs Thatcher applied the corrective in the 1980s, as the country moved more and more from its old manufacturing base over to providing services, consulting, advertising, and expertise in the 'invisible' market of high finance or in IT. Britain entertained the world with *Cats, Phantom of the Opera, Four Weddings and a Funeral, The Full Monty, Mr Bean* and the *Teletubbies.*

The post-1945 townscape has seen changes to match those in the worlds of work, entertainment and politics. In 1956 the Clean Air Act served notice on smogs and pea-souper fogs, smuts and blackened buildings, forcing people to stop burning coal and go over to smokeless sources of heat and energy. In the same decade some of the best urban building took place in the 'new towns' like Basildon, Crawley, Stevenage and Harlow. Elsewhere open warfare was declared on slums and what was labelled inadequate, cramped, back-to-back, two-up, two-down, housing. The new 'machine for living in' was a flat in a high-rise block. The architects and planners who promoted these were in league with the traffic engineers, determined to keep the motor car moving whatever the price in multi-storey car parks, meters, traffic wardens and ring roads.

Carnaby Street in the 1960s. (*Barnaby's Picture Library*)

The Millennium Dome at Greenwich, 1999. (*Michael Durnan/ Barnaby's Picture Library*)

The old pollutant, coal smoke, was replaced by petrol and diesel exhaust, and traffic noise. Even in the back garden it was hard to find peace as motor mowers, then leaf blowers and strimmers made themselves heard, and the neighbours let you share their choice of music from their powerful new amplifiers, whether you wanted to or not. Fast food was no longer only a pork pie in a pub or fish-and-chips. There were Indian curry houses, Chinese take-aways and American-style hamburgers, while the drinker could get away from beer in a wine bar. Under the impact of television the big Gaumonts and Odeons closed or were rebuilt as multi-screen cinemas, while the palais de dance gave way to discos and clubs.

From the late 1960s the introduction of listed buildings and conservation areas, together with the growth of preservation societies, put a brake on 'comprehensive redevelopment'. Now the new risk at the end of the 1990s is that town centres may die, as shoppers are attracted to the edge-of-town supermarkets surrounded by parking space, where much more than food and groceries can be bought. The ease of the one-stop shop represents the latest challenge to the good health of our towns. But with care, ingenuity and a determination to keep control of our environment, this challenge can be met.

Bristol: An Introduction

In about 1899, the Bristol Tramways & Carriage Company erected a large handsome clock on a bracket outside their offices overlooking the centre. A hundred years later it is still there: a well known landmark which has served as a meeting place for many thousands of Bristolians over the past one hundred years. But the tramway company has gone. The man who created it – and much more in the city – the aerospace industry at Filton and the modern Bristol Royal Infirmary, Sir George White, died in 1916. Since the early 1900s so much has changed in the centre and indeed, across the entire city that the survival of this clock appears all the more remarkable.

The tramway company's clock has witnessed the terror of the Blitz, the peace celebrations following two world wars and a myriad of people and traffic passing through the centre. The people have changed: they are better off, healthier and live longer as a result. There are more of them too: in 1901 the population of Bristol was 330,000 and reached a peak of 445,000 in 1955. By the end of the century a sizeable proportion had roots elsewhere in the world – in the Caribbean and the Indian sub-continent and the establishment of two universities led to a student population of 20,000 for part of the year.

The traffic has changed, too. In the early 1900s, public transport was dominated by the electric trams of the BT & CC which gathered at their triangle of raised pavement – the Tramway Centre, within sight of the clock. They also operated horse-drawn cabs: the city had a large population of working horses and goods were moved around the city in a wide variety of wagons, carts and vans. Bicycles were common but many people simply walked. In the early 1900s the city's streets were packed with traffic, but regionally and nationally roads were of limited importance. Most visitors reached the city by train or by ship – arriving at Avonmouth – or in the centre where ships docked, a short distance from shops and restaurants, offices and medieval churches.

But after the First World War, the number of motor vehicles on the road – private and commercial – increased rapidly and roads assumed a new importance. The Portway, linking the docks at Avonmouth with the city, was opened in 1926. Congestion in the centre increased as national roads such as the A4 and A38 fed their traffic into the city's narrow streets. Motorists lobbied for better roads and more parking: planners and politicians agreed and from the 1930s until the 1970s much of the old city was ripped apart to accommodate the motor car.

Conspicuously, the centre lost its stretch of open water in St Augustine's Reach to improve traffic circulation. The close physical association between the city and its port had been a distinctive feature of Bristol for centuries. By the early twentieth century, however, much of the port's business had moved to new docks at Avonmouth and Portishead, opened in the late 1870s, which were capable of taking the largest merchant ships afloat. Large extensions to the Avonmouth docks were made in 1908 and again in the 1920s and 1930s. The quaysides immediately below St Augustine's Bridge were expendable, therefore, and between 1938 and 1939 they were covered over so that this part of the City Docks became simply a part of a new inner ring road which included Temple and Redcliff Way; these new thoroughfares built in the late 1930s cut a swathe through many old properties and took a diagonal course across Queens Square. Ambitious road schemes continued to be a major feature of post-war planning and nothing was allowed to stand in their way – not even the unique eighteenth century shot tower on Redcliff Hill, demolished in 1968. In Easton, Totterdown and other parts of the older inner suburbs, hundreds of houses were cleared in the 1960s and 1970s to make way for an outer ring road. In Hotwells, Old Market, Lewins Mead and St James Barton and North Street major road re-alignments and clearances took place to make way for large roundabouts and multi-level road junctions. In or close to the centre, several large multi-storey car parks were built while the swirling mass of traffic made the centre a hostile place. In the 1970s, views on traffic priorities, however, began to change in the face of mounting public opposition to the large-scale damage caused by the road schemes. Plans for the outer ring road were abandoned, city centre parking was restricted and at the end of the century, with numbers of vehicles on the roads still increasing, motorists faced the possibility of having to pay tolls to enter the central area. And in the centre the introduction of a new traffic circulation scheme on 11 July 1999, designed to give equal consideration to other road users, replaced the 1930s road scheme and finally marked the end of the dominance of motor traffic in city centre planning.

Motor cars and buses, of course, had benefits, too: they gave people greater freedom and encouraged the development of new suburbs further from the centre. Between 1900 and the 1960s Bristol roughly doubled in size. Boundary changes resulted in Henbury, Hengrove, Withywood and Stockwood being added to the city but the population growth was not so marked and even began to fall after 1955 as people chose to live further afield outside the city boundaries in new dormitory towns such as Yate, Nailsea and Bradley Stoke. Peripheral development continued in the 1980s and 1990s with the creation of retail trading and office zones at Aztec West, Abbey Wood and Cribbs Causeway. Late twentieth century Bristol, therefore, while considerably larger than its Victorian predecessor, was less densely populated.

Road traffic was not the only factor influencing the city's development. In the 1930s there were several major clearances of old properties in the city to make way for new buildings – in College Green and Quay Head, for example, and modern style architecture made its debut: Radiant House, the gas headquarters in 1934 and the stylish Odeon cinema on the corner of Broadmead and Union Street which opened in 1938. Then enemy action wiped out large areas in the centre and several notable buildings, such as the Dutch House on the corner of Wine Street and High Street: much of the damage was done within a relatively short period of time – between 24 November 1940 and Good Friday 1941 – the period of the Blitz. Those who had pressed for modernisation before the war – local politicians, planners and architects – saw in the Blitz an opportunity to carry through a more radical reshaping of the city than would have been possible in the 1930s. Guided by the principle of zoning, in which different functions were allocated separate areas, buildings and streets which had survived the bombing were to be torn down to make way for the Broadmead shopping centre, hospital and university extensions on St Michael's Hill and the Frogmore Street entertainment centre. The City Council's planners were, in effect, creating a new city: the Evening Post described the plans as 'bold beyond the dreams of most people'. The reality, however, fell far short of the utopian vision: many old streets containing property of historical and architectural value were swept away in Kingsdown and in the Broadmead area to be replaced by drab and uninspiring new buildings. Then in the mid-1960s the City's plans – contrived and characterless – were drowned out by a boom in office building: within a brief ten year period the face and skyline of the city centre were altered irrevocably by the construction of slab and tower office blocks, some replacing fine Victorian and Edwardian commercial buildings and mocking the church towers with their sheer bulk and height. The loss of much of the city's charm and character took place to growing public opposition and by the 1970s the planners came to see the merits of conservation. From 1970, starting with

Henbury, conservation areas were designated; buildings once more came to be built – or at least faced – with brick and several historic parts of the city: Christmas Steps, buildings in Old Market and others on St Augustine's Parade, for example, were carefully restored.

There were many important changes to the city's industrial character during the twentieth century. The range and diversity of industrial production was a striking feature of the city in the early 1900s: several large and important works were situated within the central area – breweries, flour mills, iron and brass foundries – and tobacco and chocolate works – but there were also many smaller craft-based workshop industries: furniture makers, coopers, wheelwrights, saddlers and other craftsmen working in wood and leather. As the century progressed, the industrial character of the city centre diminished: some old established industries such as soap and candle making and glass working disappeared altogether, many of the smaller businesses closed – thus silk hat making, which before the First World War was carried out by five firms producing 3,000–4,000 hats annually, had dwindled to just one maker by the late 1930s, while the wheelwrights and saddlers gave way to motor garages and car dealers. Other firms relocated to new sites on the edge of the city or beyond: thus J.S. Fry & Sons left relatively modern factories around the Pithay to move to a new greenfield site at Keynsham in the 1920s; the flour mills in the City Docks moved to Avonmouth to join the zinc smelting and petro-chemical plants that had developed there from the 1920s. Notwithstanding the expansion of the Avonmouth–Severnside industrial zone, the twentieth century saw a decline in the influence of the docks on the location of new industries. The establishment of the aircraft industry at Filton owed nothing to Bristol's role as a port. The closure of the City Docks in the early 1970s to commercial traffic (except for the sand dredgers) reduced further the industrial character of the centre. Ship building ended in the City Docks in 1976 following the launch of the Miranda Guiness and by the mid 1970s the City Docks was surrounded by large tracts of derelict industrial land: roofless gas works, disused goods and transit sheds and empty timber yards. Finding alternative uses for this vital part of the city was to be a major challenge facing the city in the last quarter of the century. Industry also lost its local identity and the ties with local families, such as the Frys, the Wills and the Whites, were broken as companies were absorbed into large multi-national concerns. By the mid-1960s the existence of new links by motorway was more important, encouraging the growth of the service sector, including banking and insurance, and by the 1980s 'high-tech' industries such as computers and telecommunications.

The outward expansion of Bristol in the twentieth century involved the migration of many people from the city centre and the older suburbs to new areas of housing. In response to the Housing Act of 1919, the City Council began building new 'village suburbs' in Fishponds, Sea Mills, Bedminster, Horfield and Knowle. They were conceived as entirely new communities with their own churches, schools and shops. In 1927, Alderman Frank Shepherd, Chairman of the Housing Committee said, 'We have done our best to give people good houses set amidst picturesque surroundings' but already others were criticising the new council estates for their monotony. In the 1930s, some three thousand slum properties were cleared and their occupants rehoused; nevertheless 60 per cent of new housing built in Bristol in the inter-war period was developed by the private sector and the edges of the city acquired roads of pebble-dashed semi-detached houses built for the property-owning lower middle class. House building was interrupted by the Second World War but after 1945 the provision of new housing was the Council's top priority. With amazing speed new estates were built on farm land at Lawrence Weston, Southmead, Hartcliffe, Withywood and Stockwood. In the mid-1950s, the Council began building high rise flats on the new estates and also in the neighbourhood units established in the older suburbs – particularly in Barton Hill and Redcliff. Some areas of densely packed Victorian housing were cleared at the same time to make way for trading estates. In St Philip's Marsh, a whole community, including a church, library, shops and public houses, was obliterated, its residents relocated on the new estates. Bristol ended the century as it had begun with contrasting areas of affluence and poverty – with a buoyant north and stagnating south according to one observer in 1998 and with social problems in some districts manifested in high unemployment, struggling schools, vandalism and petty crime including car theft.

Poverty and social deprivation are, of course, relative and the fact remains that standards of living improved considerably in the twentieth century, particularly in the 1930s and 1960s. Homes acquired electricity, their occupants greater spending power with which to buy new consumer goods – first radios and electric irons, and later television sets, refrigerators and electric washing machines. Changes in consumer demand led to changes in the pattern of retailing: in the 1920s the number of national chain stores increased; in the mid-1930s tobacconists were at their peak with over 200 listed in Bristol trade directories, while shops selling radios and other electrical goods were a new feature in the main shopping centres; in the early 1960s supermarkets introduced an entirely new method of shopping and cheaper prices. Small, local shops, in many cases could not compete. They closed and people took to travelling further to new district shopping centres – at Broadwalk in Knowle, the Clifton Down shopping Centre – or to new large supermarkets built with space for hundreds of cars. The Cribbs Causeway Regional Shopping Centre, opened in April 1998, as its name implies attracts shoppers from as far away as Swindon and Cardiff, but also posed a threat to Broadmead, Bristol's postwar central shopping centre notwithstanding the opening of the Galleries there in 1991. The increase in leisure time available to people was yet another indicator of the inexorable rise in standards of living during the twentieth century. Between the beginning of the century and the 1960s working hours fell from fifty-three hours a week to forty-two. Tastes in leisure and entertainment changed and made their mark on the city: Edwardian music halls gave way to cinemas; cinemas then declined in the face of competition from television and then staged a revival in the 1990s with the opening of new large cinemas in Brislington and at Cribbs Causeway. From the 1970s the City Docks found a new role as a venue for leisure activities. At the same time foreign package holidays increasingly drew people abroad by air. Bristol remains a port: new facilities were opened at the Royal Portbury Dock in 1974 and the older docks at Avonmouth are still important but they are rarely seen by the average Bristolian and in 1991 the City Council sold the Port of Bristol to the private sector. There can be no doubt that in 1999 many Bristol people are more familiar with the departure lounge of Bristol Airport than with any part of the working dock.

Meanwhile, the former tramways clock still looks out over the city centre: traffic rushes by, people hurry past, fashions change, buildings come and go. The clock ticks on. Time never stands still.

Edwardian Bristol

Edwardian Bristol was rapidly growing and modernising. Suburban development continued across the city from Knowle to Henleaze and Avonmouth to Fishponds. Important new industries – motor bus production and aircraft manufacture – made their debut while some older established industries continued to expand. The Fry family had entered chocolate production in 1759, taking over a business started by Walter Churchman in 1728. In the first decade of the twentieth century Frys opened several new factories in the city centre but their share of the market was declining and in 1918 they merged with Cadbury although maintaining a separate identity for another sixty years.

St Augustine's Bridge, 1900. This was the centre of Bristol in 1900 – the bridge at the mouth of the culverted River Frome built in 1893 and the Tramway Centre, a triangular section of pavement, from where electric trams provided the physical link with the city's growing suburbs. The trams were operated by the privately owned Bristol Tramways & Carriage Company, whose offices were situated in the gabled building with the large clock overhanging St Augustine's Parade. To the left, the Star Assurance Building (later Dominions House) designed by the London architect, A. Bloomfield Jackson, is under construction. These buildings and the clock survived the century but much else was to go.

The centre from College Green, *c.* 1900. The beginning of the century marked the completion of the replacement of the horse-drawn trams with electric tramcars, which had first been introduced in 1895. By 22 December 1900, all extensions were worked by electricity and the following month, the BT&CC sold 345 tram horses, having no further use for them.

Redcliff Street, *c.* 1911–14. This narrow and often congested street is seen from the bottom of Redcliff Hill with Phippen Street off to the right. Redcliff Street contained a curious mix of small shops, factories and workshops producing soap, ink, starch and other goods and two large tobacco works – one belonging to W.D. & H.O. Wills and the other, visible down the street on the right, the works of Edwards, Ringer & Bigg. This imposing factory survives in 1999 but road widening schemes resulted in the demolition of virtually everything else in this view.

Old Market, *c.* 1914. Until the Second World War, Old Market was a busy and important street – effectively an eastwards extension beyond Castle Street of the city centre. It contained the Empire Theatre of Varieties, several public houses, shops, and was an important transfer point for tram services. Like so many of the older streets of the city its buildings exhibited a fascinating range of architectural styles reflecting the development of the city over many centuries.

East Street, Bedminster, *c.* 1910. Nineteenth-century expansion saw the development of new industrial communities south and east of the old city. The largest was Bedminster, with a population of 70,107 in 1901: in effect, a self-contained community with its own shopping centre running from North Street into East Street and West Street. This view is looking towards Cannon Street.

Fishponds Road, Eastville, looking east with the Capital & Counties Bank on the corner of St Marks Road. The creation of tram routes after 1875 enabled the industrial suburbs of Bristol to expand further from the centre and at the end of the nineteenth century extensive development took place in Eastville and Fishponds.

Whiteladies Road, *c.* 1910. Ornate street furniture was a feature of the the city's principal streets in the early 1900s although neither the electric arc lamp on the left nor the tram poles running down the middle of the street were then more than a few years old. On this sunny afternoon most of the shops have their window blinds unfurled, while the lady on the left shields her face from the sun with a parasol: sun tans only became fashionable from the 1920s.

Percy Kellaway, carpenter and glazier, Gloucester Road, *c.* 1910. This family business can be traced back to 1870 and was located at these premises between about 1908 and 1917. In 1921 Kellaway Avenue was named after Percy's brother, the Rt Hon. F. Kellaway, HM Postmaster-General.

Women packing Rajah cigars at W.D. & H.O. Wills, *c.* 1912. By 1901 Wills' workforce totalled 3,000, a large proportion of whom were women and girls. Frys similarly employed a large female workforce.

By 1900, there was a small but growing number of women, known as suffragettes, campaigning for the right of women to vote. In 1903 Emmeline Pankhurst and her daughters founded the Women's Social and Political Union, which advocated direct action: 'Deeds not Words' was their slogan. On 23 October 1913, they burned down the university athletic pavilion at Coombe Dingle and the next day, in retaliation, university students attacked the Bristol offices of the WSPU in Queens Road, Clifton. They broke windows and carried furniture into the street where they made a huge bonfire, watched by a cheering crowd.

William Pepworth, coal merchant, 88 Stoke Lane, Westbury-on-Trym, *c.* 1908. A variety of horse-drawn traffic filled the roads in the early part of the century: carriers' vans, four-wheeled wagons and drays and simple unsprung two-wheeled carts like this one owned by William Pepworth, who is seen on the left with his son, Bill (1902–68). The identity of the man on the right is unknown.

Loading hay at Lawrence Weston Farm, 6 July 1904. Lawrence Weston Farm comprised 128 acres rented from the Harfords of the Blaise Castle Estate; the tenant farmer was Clement Hignell, who is seen on the wagon. Some of the farms surrounding Bristol supplied the city's large population of working horses with hay and straw. The outward expansion of twentieth-century Bristol resulted in large areas of neighbouring countryside like this submerged beneath suburban developments; council houses were built on this spot after the Second World War.

Golden wedding celebrations of Canon and Mrs John Hughes Way, Henbury Vicarage, 11 July 1911. Among the guests are Mrs Harford (front row, third from left) of Blaise Castle and her daughters; most of the others are members of the Way family. The photograph provides a superb record of fashionable Edwardian dress and headgear.

Left: The Bedminster Hippodrome, East Street, *c*. 1913. The Hippodrome, with seating for 2,156, was designed by the London architect, Bertie Crewe, who had built music halls on similar lines elsewhere in Britain. Owned by Walter de Freece, the Bedminster Hippodrome opened in July 1911 but soon ran into difficulties and was taken over by Oswald Stoll, owner of the Bristol Hippodrome, on St Augustines's Parade. He converted it to a cinema in May 1915 and then in March 1918 it was renamed the Stoll Picture House. It was adapted to show talking films in 1929 but was destroyed in the Blitz.

Right: Ernest G. Hay playing the Demon in *Jack Horner*, the pantomime at the Princes Theatre, Bristol in 1913. The Princes Theatre was celebrated for its annual pantomimes from its opening in 1867 until it was destroyed in the air raid of 24 November 1940 (see page 69).

Left: Interior of the Empire Theatre of Varieties, Old Market, *c*. 1905. The Empire opened in 1893, and was designed in a distinctive Moorish style which extended to the interior decorative scheme. This was the golden age of the music hall: the Empire staged two variety shows a night with matinees on Wednesdays but soon the cinema was to erode their supremacy: Bristol's first cinema, the Bio, opened in 1908 and cinema-going quickly became all the rage; in 1933 the Empire gave up variety and was converted to a cinema. It was demolished in 1964 to make way for the widening of the inner ring road.

The King Edward Memorial building at the Bristol Royal Infirmary from a postcard, *c.* 1912. Designed by H. Percy Adams and Charles Holden (1875–1960), this can lay claim to be Bristol's first modern building. Sir George White (centre top), the energetic and far-sighted chairman of the tramway company and founder of the aeroplane works at Filton had organised the fund raising for the new building after first rescuing the hospital from major debts. The extension was opened by King George V and Queen Mary in the presence of a proud Sir George on 28 June 1912.

Fiat double-decker bus of the Bristol Tramways & Carriage Company, *c.* 1906. The BT&CC introduced its first motor bus service in January 1906 between the Victoria Rooms in Clifton and the Suspension Bridge. The first vehicles – Thornycroft double-deckers – had a top speed of 12 miles an hour; they were soon joined by a small batch of Fiats including AE 770 and from February additional services to Westbury and destinations in the surrounding countryside were introduced. In 1908 the company began the production of buses for their own use at Filton; new works at Brislington followed in 1912.

George Stanley White (1882–1964) on the box of a park drag, a four-wheeled sporting vehicle made by Fullers of Bristol outside Cotham House; one of the coachmen was called Abbott. Sir G. Stanley White was managing director of the British & Colonial Aeroplane Company – later the Bristol Aeroplane Company – from 1911 until 1958. During that period he saw aircraft production at Filton progress from the wood, cotton and wire of the Bristol Boxkite to the stainless steel Bristol Type 188 capable of flying at twice the speed of sound.

A 15 horse-power Panhard Levassor of 1903 given by Sir George White to his son G. Stanley White as a twenty-first birthday present, seen here at the family home, Cotham House, with its registration plate of AE10. Dating from 1905, the year car registrations were introduced in Bristol, this is the oldest surviving Bristol motor car to retain its original number plate.

In February 1910, Sir George White established his aeroplane company using factory premises leased from the tramway company at Filton. By November 1910 Bristol Biplanes – or 'Boxkites' – were being built at the rate of two a week and two well-known French pilots, Henri M. Jullerot and Maurice Tétard, were engaged to test them. On 14 November, in damp and overcast weather, crowds of people watched as Jullerot took off from the Downs and flew over the Clifton Suspension Bridge – just visible here in the gloom. Few people can then have imagined the impact that aviation was to have on the twentieth century and particularly in Bristol where the Filton-based company was to become the single largest employer by the mid-century.

The entrance hall at Cotham House, the home of Sir George White (1854–1916), *c.* 1904. Between 1889 and 1915 Sir George lavished a fortune refitting and furnishing the house, employing the Bristol architect George Oatley (later Sir George) and buying modern furniture, mostly, but in a period style. By 1904 the contents and works of art were valued at £60,000.

The First World War

Tommy's ABC, issued by the Bristol branch of the British Red Cross Society in 1916. The Bristol branch had been founded by Sir George White and Charles Thomas was a local illustrator and cartoonist. The *Clifton Free Press* wrote of this booklet, 'The pictures are full of fun, excellently drawn and printed. We think it a ripping book, worth double the money'. It sold for one shilling and profits went to Red Cross funds.

Wine Street, looking towards the High Street, some time between 1915 and 1919. Wine Street, along with Castle Street, formed Bristol's chief shopping centre and contained many of the city's most exclusive shops and department stores. This view was taken after March 1915 when the globes and lanterns of street lamps were painted blue to dim their light as an air raid precaution. In the event Bristol suffered no attacks from German aircraft during the First World War but twenty-five years later it was very different and during the first night of the Blitz on 24 November 1940 this thoroughfare was almost completely destroyed.

Bristol Bridge from the High Street, between 1915 and 1919. Another wartime view with the lamps on the bridge painted blue. On the left a tram bound for Brislington stops to pick up passengers, while on the right a no. 10 service from Knowle ends its journey at the bridge. The imposing and ornate Robinson building of 1876 dominates the corner of Victoria Street: it was badly damaged during the Blitz of 1940–1 but survived until 1961 when it was demolished to make way for the new Robinson tower block (see page 102).

The sailing ship, *Elfrieda*, moored at Mardyke, *c.* 1915. By the early 1900s, the majority of ships entering the City Docks were steamships: of the 515 ships registered upon arrival in the City Docks in 1914, only seventeen were sailing vessels. One was the *Elfrieda*: she had arrived on fire under a German flag on 21 May 1914 with a cargo of wheat from Sydney for Spillers and Bakers. Her repairs probably delayed her departure and at the outbreak of war she was seized and her crew placed under detention; however, as her officers were over military age they were allowed to return home and the ship finally set sail on 27 May 1915. The iron-hulled *Elfrieda*, 261 ft long, had been built as the *Chrisomene* in Liverpool in 1873.

The naval company of the National Reserve, 1914. The company is seen here in Jamaica Street about to start on a recruiting march. The Bristol branch of the National Reserve – originally called the Veteran Reserve – had been formed late in 1910 and consisted of four companies plus this naval company.

The 4th Battalion (City of Bristol) Gloucesters, No. 2 Company, in the grounds of Bristol Grammar School in 1914. The number of would-be recruits in the first few days of the war was enough to form several battalions. Bristol Grammar School voluntarily gave up its playing field in Tyndall's Park for army training. Altogether some 60,000 Bristolians enlisted for armed service during the First World War and 4,000 were killed.

The 12th Battalion of the Gloucestershire Regiment, 'Bristol's Own', undergoing physical training at Ashton Gate, 1914–15. This battalion was established on 4 September 1914 as part of Kitchener's New Army. Recruits had to be unmarried and aged between nineteen and thirty-five. In less than a fortnight, 500 recruits – practically half the battalion's full strength – had been enrolled and at once became known as 'Bristol's Own'. The initial training of the new recruits took place through the winter of 1914–15 and on 21 November 1915 they crossed to France and saw action in the area of the Somme.

B and D Company of the Black Watch marching to Temple Meads en route to Sutton Veney, Wiltshire. B Company stationed at the Victoria Rooms and D Company at the Coliseum met at the top of Park Street.

University students march past the Hope and Anchor public house in Jacobs Wells Road on their way to camp at Barrow, 7 September 1914.

As men were called up to serve in the armed services, women and girls took their place in factories and offices. From 1 January 1917, the Bristol Tramways & Carriage Company followed the example of other large tram operators and started employing young women between the ages of eighteen and twenty-five as tram conductors. One was Elise Shepstone, seen here wearing a warm winter coat. In April 1920 following hostile and disorderly protests from unemployed ex-servicemen the company was compelled to dismiss them; they were given a week's notice and a £5 gratuity. Nevertheless, the role of working women during the war undoubtedly assisted the cause for universal suffrage. In 1918 The Representation of the People Act gave the vote to women householders, the wives of householders and graduates over 30 and in 1928 all women over 21 became eligible to vote.

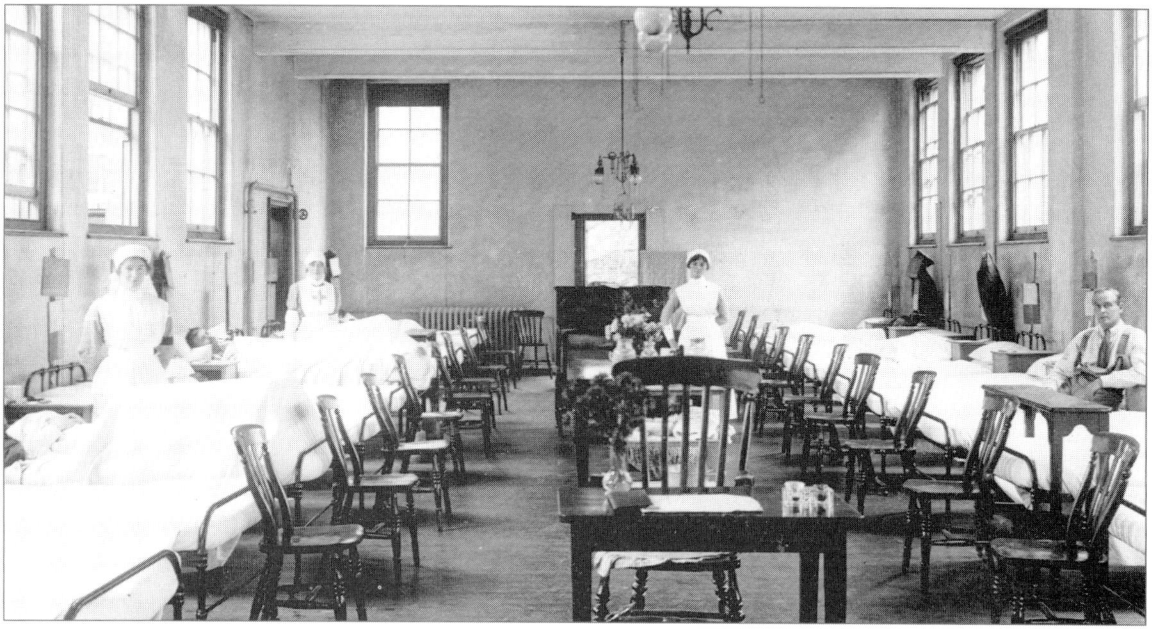

The Ypres Ward, Red Maids Hospital, Westbury-on-Trym, *c.* 1917. The Bristol branch of the Red Cross arranged for the use of the new wing of the Bristol Royal Infirmary to be used as a base hospital from the outset of war while Southmead Hospital became part of the 2nd Southern General Hospital. Subsequently, further auxiliary hospitals were established by the British Red Cross Society and in 1916 the Red Maids School at Westbury-on-Trym was converted into a hospital containing 200 beds.

First gathering of the wounded in the Soldiers' Room at Bristol Museum, 26 October 1916. The first wounded soldiers – 120 men from Mons – arrived in Bristol on 2 September 1914 and from then until the end of the war 69,411 injured soldiers were treated in Bristol.

A tea party for injured soldiers recovering at the Bristol Royal Infirmary. The location is not given but the soldiers convalescing at the BRI were frequently taken on cruises to tea gardens on the Avon. In 1915 alone a total of 11,773 sick and wounded soldiers arrived in Bristol from the fronts in France, Belgium and Gallipoli.

Artists and staff involved in a special matinee for wounded soldiers held at the Bristol Hippodrome, 18 June 1915. Standing (left to right): H. Galpin, the conductor, L. Le Sine, G. Jackley, R.A. Speedwell, Macdonald Watson, R. Drysdale, Frank Bent, the press manager and J. Gosgrove. Seated: Mark Sheridan, Miss Nell Barke, Miss 'Sonia', Edward Fryer, the assistant manager, Miss Beryl Clifford, Mr 'Samaroff' and Wee Georgie Wood.

Wounded soldiers on a trip by steamer to Saltford, *c.* 1917.

Germany surrendered on Monday 11 November 1918 and spontaneous celebrations broke out across the city. A month later two captured German submarines were towed into the City Docks and put on public show in St Augustine's Reach. German submarines had inflicted heavy losses on Allied shipping during the war, including merchant shipping and hospital ships on their way to Bristol.

The year 1919 was a difficult one: the war was over but unemployment was rising – so were prices – and in January, a serious influenza epidemic caused many deaths. But 19 July was appointed as the day for national peace celebrations and in Bristol a procession of thousands of demobilised soldiers, veterans from the Crimean War and the Indian Mutiny, led by mounted police, made their way from Queens Square to Durdham Down. The day was marred by heavy rain and many in the crowds seen here at the Tramway Centre are holding umbrellas.

Between the Wars

Park Row, *c.* 1937. The Wills Memorial tower designed by the Bristol architect Sir George Oatley was opened by King George V and Queen Mary on 9 June 1925. Here the tower is seen from Park Row with the Coliseum on the right which had opened as one of Bristol's earliest cinemas in August 1912. The tram is on its way to Durdham Down.

The Tramway Centre, *c.* 1937. Trams on services to Filton, Kingswood and Durdham Down via Zetland Road line up on the triangular pavement in the city centre in front of the handsome Sun Life Insurance building of 1902, designed by Sir George Oatley and demolished in 1971. One of the double decker buses which had been reintroduced by the Bristol Tramways & Carriage Company in 1931 and which were soon to replace the trams altogether in the centre is just visible on the extreme left; before the war the company's buses shared the same attractive dark blue and ivory livery as their trams.

By this date the volume of motor traffic in the centre was causing serious congestion: two national trunk roads – the A4 linking Avonmouth with London and the A38 from the Midlands to the South West – intersected here and are indicated on the road sign on the right; nine other main roads also converged on the centre. In November 1935 the City Council approved a scheme prepared by the Planning and Public Works and Improvement Committee to construct a new western road – or inner ring road – between St Augustine's Parade and Victoria Street to reduce the volume of traffic in the centre and provide a more direct route to the railway station at Temple Meads. The new road involved bridging the harbour about 150 yards below St Augustine's Bridge, then cutting diagonally across Queen's Square before crossing the Floating Harbour by a new bascule bridge by Redcliff Wharf. Work began the following year and in September 1936 the Western Daily Press reported that workmen had begun stripping back the turf in Queens Square leaving a 'long black gash' while massive old trees were uprooted for the new road.

The Centre viewed from the CWS building, *c.* 1930. This was the scene that so fascinated J.B. Priestley when he visited the centre of Bristol in 1933: 'a place' he wrote, 'where trams and coastal steamers seemed in danger of a collision'. The close proximity of the working dock to the centre is clearly evident here with crates and barrels lying outside the Dublin transit shed in the foreground – just yards away from shops on Broad Quay and from the trams, of course, at their triangular centre above St Augustine's Bridge.

By the end of the decade this view had radically changed: the construction of the new road from St Augustine's Parade across the dock 150 yards below St Augustine's Bridge rendered the intervening stretch of quayside redundant. The Dublin shed was demolished in 1936 and in July 1937 plans were released for covering over the water to create, in the words of *The Times* on 20 July 1937, 'a magnificent avenue' to be called King George V Memorial Avenue. Ornamental gardens and fountains were to occupy the central space bounded by the new roads and in the middle a 60-ft high memorial tower surmounted by a lantern was to have been erected. The culverting of the dock was completed by the time war was declared in 1939 but the landscaping had to wait another ten years and then it was a much simplified version of the original scheme: the memorial theme was dropped – and with it the fountains and lantern tower; the central garden island went ahead but this was removed in the spring of 1999 to make way for another major remodelling of the centre.

The Tramway Centre, mid-1930s. A lively evening scene after dark in the centre with the bright lights of the Hippodrome, shops, cafés and restaurants on St Augustine's Parade overlooking the trams as they clatter around their triangular island immediately above St Augustine's Bridge. The electric trams carried thousands of people a day between the suburbs and the centre, but services had not adapted and expanded to meet the continuing growth of the city: no new routes had been added since 1908 and some of the new council estates such as Sea Mills were beyond the existing network. By the 1930s trams, generally, were seen as old-fashioned. A report published in 1931 by the Royal Commission on Transport stated trams were: 'in a state of obsolescence' and caused unnecessary congestion and considerable unnecessary danger to the public. Moreover, the Bristol Tramways & Carriage Company still relied on the original fleet of open-topped trams, which, roughly forty years old looked decidedly old-fashioned compared to the fully enclosed trams used by many other operators. So in the late 1930s, Bristol followed the example of towns and cities elsewhere in Britain and decided to do away with its trams. The replacement with buses began in 1938: tram services from the centre were discontinued after 15 July 1939 and elsewhere in the city in April 1941.

St Stephens House, corner of St Stephens Avenue and Quay Street, 1939. The large-scale redevelopment which occurred in Bristol after the Second World War and particularly in the 1960s and early 1970s can obscure the fact that several large important buildings were added to the centre in the inter-war period. Northcliffe House, the offices of the *Evening World* newspaper, was completed in Colston Avenue in 1929 and in 1936 work began on the building of Electricity House – headquarters of the City Council's Electricity Department on an island site bounded by Rupert Street, Nelson Street and Christmas Street. Although not completed until after the Second World War, Electricity House, designed by Sir Giles Scott was intended to set the style for other large impressive buildings in the centre – befitting an important regional city.

Radiant House, the headquarters of the gas company in Colston Street, introduced modern style motifs to the centre in 1935 with its curved glass windows and equally striking was the Odeon cinema opened in 1938, which made the most of its corner site at the junction of Union Street and Broadmead with an art deco inspired tower. St Stephen's House was designed by Alec French and completed in 1939. The use of black tiles around the corner entrance contrasts with the white Portland stone walls but lacking the curves of Radiant House and the Odeon the building appears rather severe. Nevertheless, the building formed new prestigious offices for the Bristol & West Building Society, reflecting the society's growth and prosperity in the 1920s and 1930s in response to the rising popularity of home ownership. Between 1918 and 1939 the total assets of the society rose from £290,000 to £4.2 million; however, it still ranked only thirty-fourth in size nationally in 1939 and had just three branches – in Bedminster, Gloucester Road and one in Exeter.

St Peter's Hospital, 1930s. Night-time photographs of buildings lit by floodlight were fashionable in the 1930s: here the technique shows to perfection the ornate timber-framed St Peter's Hospital close by St Peter's Church. Originally dating from the fifteenth century, the house was rebuilt by Robert Aldworth, a prominent citizen in 1612. After serving as a mint during the recoinage of 1696–8, it was used as a hospital for lunatics and the destitute, ending up as the Register Office. It was destroyed in the first night of the Blitz on Sunday 24 November 1940.

The Dutch House, corner of High Street and Wine Street, 1930s. In the thirties this was one of Bristol's favourite tourist attractions occupying a commanding city centre site: a picturesque timber-framed structure with a romantic past – it was widely believed to have been prefabricated in Holland and brought over to Bristol in the 1690s. In reality, it was built on this site in 1676, and not in Holland. The Dutch connection was a Victorian myth: it was then heavily altered in 1909 to allow for road widening. It was, nevertheless, a building of considerable charm and character and its loss in the Blitz was a sad one for Bristol.

30 Baldwin Street, *c.* 1935. This building was the premises of the Bristol Development Board, established in 1929 and financed jointly by local industrialists and the City Council to promote the city and the port; it was taken over by the City Council in 1947. The street level shop is occupied by Dickin and Green, tobacconists: nationally, consumption of tobacco almost doubled in this decade: smoking was fashionable, chic and believed to promote good health. By 1999, it was very different and the number of specialist tobacconists in the city had dropped to just four. A Rover is parked outside the shop.

Spear Brothers & Clark Ltd, English Bacon Curers, 36 Victoria Street, decorated for the Coronation of George VI, March 1937.

Platform 9, Temple Meads station, *c.* 1938. In 1930 work commenced on a major rebuilding of the station, which was completed in December 1935.

Aerial view of the entrance to the City Docks at Cumberland Basin, late 1920s. A ship leaves the Cumberland Basin by the North Entrance Lock. Vessels continued to enter the Floating Harbour via the New Cut at Bathurst Basin until 1934. The A38 crosses the cut by the Ashton swing bridge and then the Cumberland Basin at Junction Lock Bridge. The Great Western Railway branch from Ashton Junction to the Canons Marsh goods depot crossed on the lower deck of the Ashton swing bridge and then crossed the Cumberland Basin by a narrow swing bridge which can be seen behind the road bridge. Stothert's ship yard continued to occupy the dry dock of Merchants Dock until 1933.

The Bristol General Hospital from the Bathurst Basin, *c.* 1930. The General Hospital had occupied this corner site overlooking the Bathurst Basin since 1862. A large extension (right) was added in 1912 but the hospital suffered damage in the Blitz and the cupola surmounting the corner tower was removed. The Bathurst Basin connected the Floating Harbour with the New Cut but the lock gates were blocked off during the Second World War. The depot of the Holmes Sand & Gravel Co. was located in the basin and their vessel the *Alwin*, built in 1902 and converted to sand sucking in 1924, is moored at their berth. The *Alwin* remained in Bristol until about 1950 and was scrapped in 1960.

Avonmouth Docks, March 1936. Hosegood's mills overlooking the original dock of 1877 is nearing completion while the Elders & Fyffes vessel, *Cefalu*, unloads her cargo of Jamaican bananas at N berth. The importation of West Indian bananas had begun in 1901 and at this time roughly a third of all bananas entering the country came through Avonmouth: banana vans belonging to the Great Western railway and the London Midland & Scottish Railway occupy the railway sidings. The *Wearwood*, on the right, had arrived from Rosario, Argentina, with a cargo of grain on 20 March. The King Edward Dock of 1908 which had just recently been extended is to the right, and the River Avon is visible on the left.

Stevedores unloading grain at Avonmouth, 1930s. From the 1920s the Port invested in mechanical handling equipment but the unloading of cargoes remained labour intensive until the advent of containerisation in the 1960s. A casual workforce of some 3,000 dockers was employed by the Port at this time and large groups of dockers unloading loose cargoes were an essential part of the docks scene.

Portishead power station, *c.* 1930. In 1901 the use of electricity in the city was still in its infancy: municipally controlled supplies were first generated in 1893 from works at Temple Back. In 1902 a second power station – the Avonbank Electricity Works – on Feeder Road opened and by 1911 there were 3,600 users. Growing demand in the 1920s led to the construction of this power station by the City Council on a 23-acre site at Portishead, which was commissioned in 1929. The domestic consumption of electricity increased rapidly and by 1935 there were 71,935 users – over 63 per cent of all households in the city.

The production line of Bristol Bulldogs at the Bristol Aeroplane Company's Works, Filton, *c.* 1930. The Bulldog made its first flight on 17 May 1927 and quickly established a reputation for excellent manoeuvrability; it was a star performer in the great air shows of the 1930s and at one time constituted 70 per cent of Britain's fighter air defence.

Tyreing a cartwheel at Fivash, wheelwrights and farriers, St Thomas Street, October 1937. By the 1930s the highly skilled craft of making wooden cartwheels by hand was fast disappearing. In this view the red-hot iron tyre is being placed around the wooden rim of the wheel; moments later it will be drenched in cold water to shrink it on to the wheel.

City Motors, Quakers Friars, *c.* 1938. In the 1920s and '30s motor car dealers and repair garages grew in numbers as car owners increased. City Motors was established in about 1930 at King Street and by 1932 had these premises at Quakers Friars, which curiously incorporated a Perpendicular style window of the fifteenth century, discovered in 1933.

Until the construction of new works at Somerdale, Keynsham in the 1920s and early 1930s most of the Frys works were concentrated on a cramped two-and-a-half acre site site bounded by Union Street, Nelson Street and Tower Lane. This 1936 view shows two factories located either side of Duck Lane: number 3 with its chimney stack on the right and number 4, which was dated 1885, on the left. Number 3 factory was demolished in 1937 to make way for the development of the Odeon cinema but number 4, which backed onto Gardiner & Sons premises in Nelson Street, survived until 1961, its chimney being demolished in January of that year.

Cecil R. Fry, Chairman of J.S. Fry & Sons (left, seated) and Miss E.J.A. Phillips (left foreground), who was responsible for organising guided tours of the works are seen at Frys, Union Street, on 19 September 1924 with members of the D'Oyly Cart Opera Company including Bristol born singer, Elsie Griffin (second row, second from right with the bouquet of flowers). Elsie Griffin was born in Bristol and when young sang in the choir at Lewins Mead Chapel. She later became a principal with the Carl Rosa Opera Company.

Three months later, on 14 December 1924, Prince George paid a brief visit to Frys, Union Street, 14 December 1924. The presence of twelve press photographers clearly added to the discomfort of the shy young Prince as he tastes liquid chocolate drawn from a 'melangeur' – a large mixing machine – offered to him by Miss E.J.A. Phillips while a proud Cecil Fry looks on.

Drawing the boilers at Fry's number 7 factory between the Pithay and Tower Lane for the last time on 31 August 1935. The factory was sold in 1938 and demolished in 1964.

Prices Bottle Co., *c.* 1937. Stoneware bottle manufacture in Bristol dated from the early eighteenth century and Prices business from 1796 but it was brought to an abrupt end by the Blitz in November 1940. Thirty years later, collecting old bottles emerged as a new hobby and bottles like these became highly sought after by collectors.

Georges' Brewery, May 1937. The brewery is seen here decorated with buntings for the Coronation of King George VI. Georges & Co. was Bristol's largest brewery, having absorbed many smaller rivals in the city in the late nineteenth century. Largest of these was the Bristol United Brewery, based in Lewins Mead, which it took over in 1956.

White Hart Hotel, corner of Upper Maudlin Street and Terrell Street, *c.* 1938. Georges' name was found on many public houses in the city until the company was absorbed by Courages in 1961. In the 1930s the company owned over 900 licensed premises in the Bristol area. There were also pubs tied to local breweries, but only a few free houses.

Loading a Commer van at the Golden Shred Works of James Robertson & Sons, Water Lane, Brislington, *c.* 1939. From the early twentieth century new industrial zones developed beyond the city centre. Brislington was one and by the 1930s several engineering and food processing firms had established works here. Robertson's jam factory dated from about 1914 and closed in August 1980.

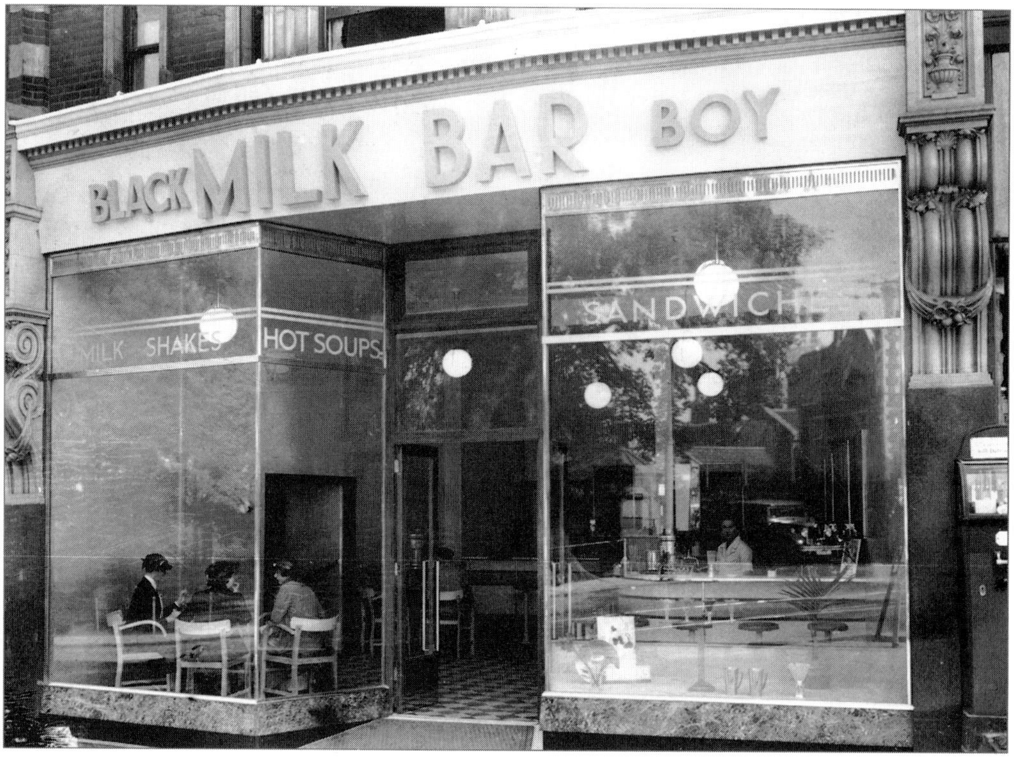

In the 1930s modern art deco styles began to influence the design and layout of shops, cafés and restaurants. Chrome, plate glass and sans-serif lettering sometimes illuminated in neon lights began to replace the gas-lit shop fronts fashionable in the late Victorian and Edwardian period. The Blackboy Milk Bar is the very epitome of late 1930s modernism yet retains the heavy carved brackets of an earlier shop front. In 1999, the premises are occupied by an Indian restaurant, the plate-glass windows have gone but the brackets, painted bright blue, survive!

Willsons Ladies Outfitters, 72 and 73 Castle Street, *c.* 1933. This business was established in 1933 in Castle Street, one of the principal city centre shopping streets of pre-war Bristol. By the end of the decade, Willsons had modernised their façade with a cleaner Art Deco style frontage than the one recorded here. The windows are covered with posters advertising a fashion competition organised by the *Evening World* newspaper, which was printed in Bristol from 1929 to 1962.

Bristol Co-operative Society store, Gloucester Road, mid-1930s. The Bristol & District Co-operative Society had been formed in 1884 by a group of trade unionists to give members a share of the profits on the sale of the 'necessaries' of life. By the mid-1930s the Bristol society owned fifty-two grocery, confectionery and greengrocery branches, including this one in Gloucester Road, and members were paid a dividend of 1*s* 8*d* for every £1 spent in the shops.

Above: Kingsland Road, St Phillips, 22 January 1925. The building of new council houses in Fishponds, Sea Mills and Bedminster after 1919 did little to solve the problem of slums and many sub-standard properties remained occupied in the 1920s, especially in the inner city and in the older suburbs such as St Phillips and Bedminster. In 1933, responding to national legislation, the City Council approved a programme for the clearance of 2,900 slum properties; the occupants were rehoused in new council houses built in Bedminster and Knowle.

Left: Entrance to a disused slaughterhouse, 19 Frogmore Street, 1928. In February 1928, the *Western Daily Press* reported that Frogmore Street could lay claim to possessing more unsavoury courts than any other street in Bristol. Warren's Court, off Frogmore Street, was one of the blackest spots and contained a dwelling of two rooms inhabited by nine people. Like the entrance to this slaughter house they were all reached by a narrow passage way. Such picturesque alley ways and courts added to the variety and charm of the city but were tidied up or demolished altogether in the middle decades of the century while most of the worst slums were cleared in the 1930s.

Pims Court, Horsefair, *c.* 1933. Damp, crowded and insanitary, slums nevertheless made compelling subjects for the camera. This small enclosed court was located behind the Lower Arcade and reached through Wesley Court. The yard paving is in a poor state and some of the window-panes are cracked and broken. A gas lamp illuminates the corner of the building and the Council's slum clearance notice is stuck to the wall between the two ground floor windows. The site of this court is now a small open space in front of Wesley's New Rooms.

Corner of Filton Road and Gregory Road, *c.* 1930. Bristol's first council house was built in Fishponds in 1919 and through the 1920s and 1930s new estates were established on greenfield sites, mostly on the edge of the city. By 1939, some 14,500 new council houses had been built in Bristol, pushing the boundaries of suburban Bristol ever further outwards and creating a new environment of working-class suburbs. These houses are on the Horfield estate, developed from the mid-1920s on land between Filton Road and the railway line running northwards from Temple Meads to Filton: the houses in St Gregory Road were built in 1925.

Council house garden, possibly in Fishponds, 1930s. The council estates created an entirely new environment, a world apart from the densely packed Victorian suburbs and inner city slums. The layout of the estates was inspired by the garden city movement: houses were given generous sized gardens front and back and the Council encouraged tenants to use their gardens – particularly to grow vegetables. Annual competitions were staged for the best-kept garden and this photograph of a neat and well-tended garden is an unidentified prizewinner of the 1930s.

The Second World War

Programme cover for the 'Bristol Salutes the Soldier Week' which took place between 13 and 20 May 1944 – shortly before the D-Day landings in Normandy.

Sir George S.M. White (1913–83), grandson of the first Sir George White – founder of the Bristol Aeroplane Company and later the chairman and managing director of Bristol Cars – is seen reviewing the Bristol Aeroplane Company's own fire brigade at the Filton works during the war.

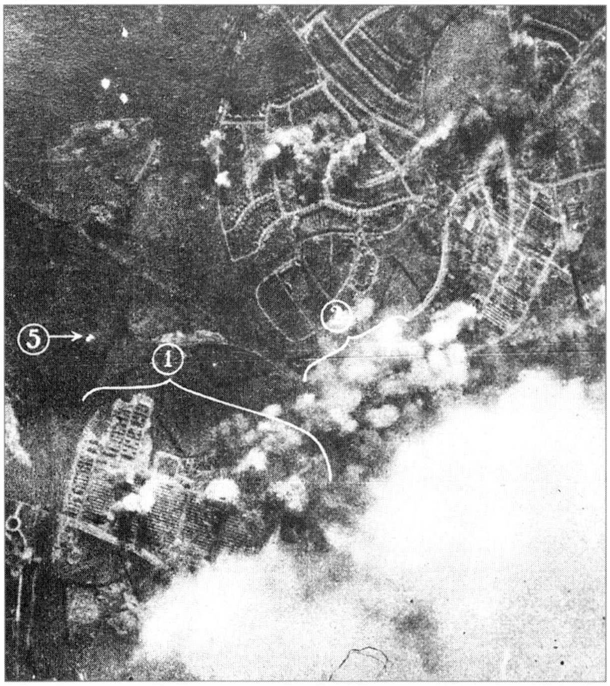

A Luftwaffe photograph of the bombing of the aeroplane works at Filton, 25 September 1940. Several minor raids occurred through the summer of 1940 but the first serious one took place on the morning of 25 September when German aircraft reached Filton and within 45 seconds inflicted heavy damage on the aircraft plant: ninety-one employees of the company were killed and the development of the Beaufighter was delayed. During the raid anti-aircraft gunners at Portishead succeeded in shooting down a Heinkel bomber – one of only two enemy aircraft brought down in the Bristol area during the Second World War.

Queen Mary took a particular interest in the war effort made by the Bristol Aeroplane Company and made many visits to the Filton works when she was staying with the Duke of Beaufort at Badminton: doubtless, the need to follow royal etiquette meant that everything ground to a standstill during her visits!

King George VI and Queen Elizabeth inspect a Bristol Blenheim fighter on a visit to Filton during the war. An RAF Blenheim was the first aircraft to cross the German frontier – just 48 minutes after the Prime Minister's radio broadcast announcing the declaration of war.

Air raid wardens pose for the camera at the Crescent, Henleaze, *c.* 1941. The Second World War brought the civilian population into direct contact with the enemy and people participated in the defence of the city through voluntary bodies such as the air raid wardens and street fire guards. Bristol's civil defence was co-ordinated by the ARP based in Broadmead, which was under the direct control of the Chief Constable.

Bristol Beaufighter. The Beaufighter made its first flight on 17 July 1939 and by the time production ended in early 1944, 5,564 had been made in England and 364 in Australia.

Bomb damage in Bridge Street, November 1940. The church of St Mary-le-Port was destroyed although the tower, seen here, survived. Twenty-eight churches and chapels were completely destroyed and 156 damaged by enemy action in the war, while 487 shops were lost in the centre.

The first major night raid of 24 November 1940 destroyed the Dutch House occupied by the Irish Linen and Hosiery Association

The Princes Theatre, Park Row after the raid of 24 November 1940. The ruins were only finally removed in November 1964.

West Street, Bedminster, 1941. The older suburbs also suffered in the Blitz. This was all that was left of tramcar no. 9 after a bomb fell on West Street near Chessel Road in January 1941.

Daylight air raid on Broad Weir, 28 August 1942. By 1942 the worst of the Blitz was over but on a clear weekday morning in August 1942, as people were going to work, a Junkers Ju86R flying largely undetected at high altitude, dropped a single high explosive bomb which struck Broad Weir setting fire to three buses loaded with passengers and killing forty-five people. Altogether, 1,250 Bristolians were killed in the war, a further 3,000 were injured and 89,000 properties were destroyed. Not surprisingly, this disturbing image was withheld from publication at the time.

A group of US soldiers are photographed outside old Filton House in April 1943 – although these are actually all Bristolians: there are about twenty places called Bristol in the United States and these soldiers came from some of them.

Sir Frederick Pyle opens the first 'Airoh' prefabricated house made by the Bristol Aeroplane Company at Shirehampton, 18 July 1945. Over 3,000 temporary homes were erected in Ashton Vale, Sea Mills, Westbury-on-Trym and elsewhere in the city; they proved popular and 800 prefabs survive in the city in 1999 of which 100 are privately owned.

Victory tea party in the Muller Road area, Eastville, 1945. On VE-Day – 8 May 1945 – people celebrated the end of the war with street parties and tea parties for children like this one in Eastville. Denis Williams, whose photographs of Cary Grant in Bristol some 20 years later appear on page 105, is the twenty-first from the front on the the right-hand side; he was then aged eight. His neighbours, Shirley Hall and Jean King, are in the foreground on the left.

The Postwar Period

Before the war was over, the City Council began planning a radical reshaping of the city: it was to be reorganised into separate zones for civic use, shopping, health, education and entertainment. Industry was to move to new suburban locations where factories, schools and recreational facilities would be grouped in 'neighbourhood units'. In the immediate post-war years the building of new homes and schools were the Council's chief priorities. The reconstruction formed the subject of an exhibition entitled 'Bristol – Gateway to the West' mounted for the Festival of Britain in 1951. It included displays on a wide range of council functions including planning, housing, education, health, libraries and street lighting. In this publicity photograph artwork for the exhibition is being prepared. Zoning as a planning philosophy ultimately fell from favour but its lasting legacy is the Broadmead shopping centre, the post-war housing estates at Redcliff, Lawrence Weston and Hartcliffe, and the university and hospital extensions on St Michael's Hill.

A large crowd witnesses the naming ceremony of the Bristol Brabazon at Filton, 8 October 1947. This aeroplane was commissioned by a government committee established in 1942, chaired by Lord Brabazon, to identify Britain's post-war aviation needs. Its production was a considerable achievement for the Bristol Aeroplane Company as it was considerably larger and more technically advanced than anything it had previously built and when the Brabazon made its maiden flight, on 4 October 1949, it was the largest civil aircraft in the world.

Bill Pegg, the Chief Test Pilot of the Bristol Aeroplane Company, poses for the camera at Filton alongside the Bristol Brabazon and a Bristol 400 two-litre car, *c.* 1949. The Brabazon was designed by Sir Archibald Russell, who also designed the Bristol Britannia and led the the British design team on Concorde. Before a second prototype could be completed, however, it was evident that the future in long-haul civil aviation lay with jet propulsion and in 1952 the project was abandoned and the following year this handsome aeroplane was scrapped.

The aeroplane works received visits from many famous names throughout the twentieth century. Here a superb photograph of about 1950 captures the American film actress, Joan Fontaine (centre), with Bill Pegg, the Chief Test Pilot and Mrs Vera Thomas, the widow of Herbert Thomas, formerly a director of the company, who had died in about 1948. Joan Fontaine was a frequent guest of the Thomases and as befitting a Hollywood star was always accompanied by a large entourage.

A Bristol freighter seemingly devours its cargo through its nose door in a publicity photograph of the late 1940s. This aircraft started life towards the end of the Second World War as a military aircraft but enjoyed success as a civil freight carrier and production totalled 214. By 1999, however, only one example survived.

Air Marshal Sir Thomas Walker Elmhurst, Chief of Air Staff, and Lady Elmhust admire a Bristol 401 with a 400 model behind them at Filton, 9 May 1949. The car division of the Bristol Aeroplane Company was established after the Second World War and gained a reputation for expensive luxury cars based on in-house expertise in aircraft design and from drawings belonging to the German manufacturers, BMW, confiscated after the war. The first model, the 400, made its debut in 1947 and the 401 two years later.

Park Street, *c.* 1950. While new aircraft and luxury cars gave an air of glamour to the Bristol Aeroplane Company's Filton works, much of the city bore a shabby and neglected appearance with many derelict bomb sites and damaged buildings. Park Street, one of the city's most prestigious shopping streets, had several gaps due to wartime bombing although work had resumed on completing the Council House; a sign belonging to William Cowlin & Son, the main contractors, faces the street. The buses approaching the camera are in the new post-war green and cream livery.

Victoria Street, *c.* 1950. This important thoroughfare connecting the city centre with Temple Meads station had suffered badly in the Blitz and some of the gaps are evident in this view. More of the original commercial buildings built in the 1870s were to go in the 1950s and 1960s and at the end of the century only a few restored examples survived to give some idea of the former grandeur of the Italianate style offices and showrooms of polychrome brick which originally lined the street.

The Council House, *c.* 1956. Designed by E. Vincent Harris, the new Council House was actually a pre-war design begun in 1935, which was intended to provide the council with more spacious and prestigious offices. Its completion delayed by the Second World War, it was formally opened by Elizabeth II on 17 May 1956 but its severe neo-Georgian façade and flat landscaped lawn in front has attracted criticism.

The Housing Committee, 1957. The building of new houses was carried out by the Housing Committee at a prodigious rate in the post-war period and between 1948 and 1951 more new permanent homes were built in Bristol than in any other authority, London excluded. By the end of 1972, 33,461 council homes had been built within the city since the war. In 1957 the Chairman of the Housing Committee was W.J. Waring.

Whitehouse Lane, Bedminster, *c.* 1950. Victorian terraced houses in Whitehouse Lane, part of a thriving community between York Road and the railway line to the south-west, which was cleared in the 1950s and 1960s to make way for the Bedminster Trading Estate, are seen here; similar houses were cleared about the same time in St Phillips Marsh for more light industrial and commercial premises.

Redcliff goods yard, *c.* 1950. Evidence of the survival into the 1950s of horse-drawn road vehicles is seen in this view of Redcliff goods yard taken from the roof of St Mary Redcliff. Two flat wagons and a covered van are parked alongside the track but they would soon be a thing of the past: British Railways withdrew their horses from the streets in 1953 and from goods yards in 1962. The Redcliff yard closed in January 1964.

Council flats, New Street, St Jude's, 1950s. This photograph was taken after the flats had been refurbished by the council.

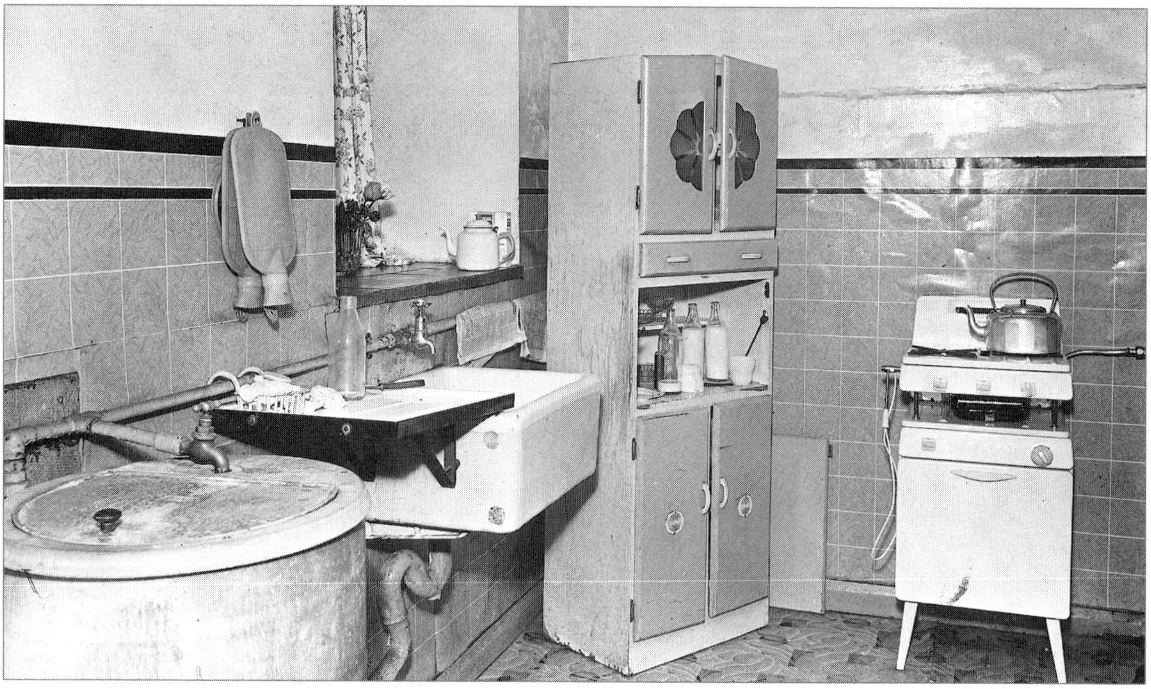

Kitchen, New Street flats, St Jude's, mid-1950s. Recorded before council improvements were carried out, this kitchen was typical of thousands in Bristol in the post-war period with its gas cooker and gas boiler for clothes washing, a free-standing kitchen cabinet and Belfast sink.

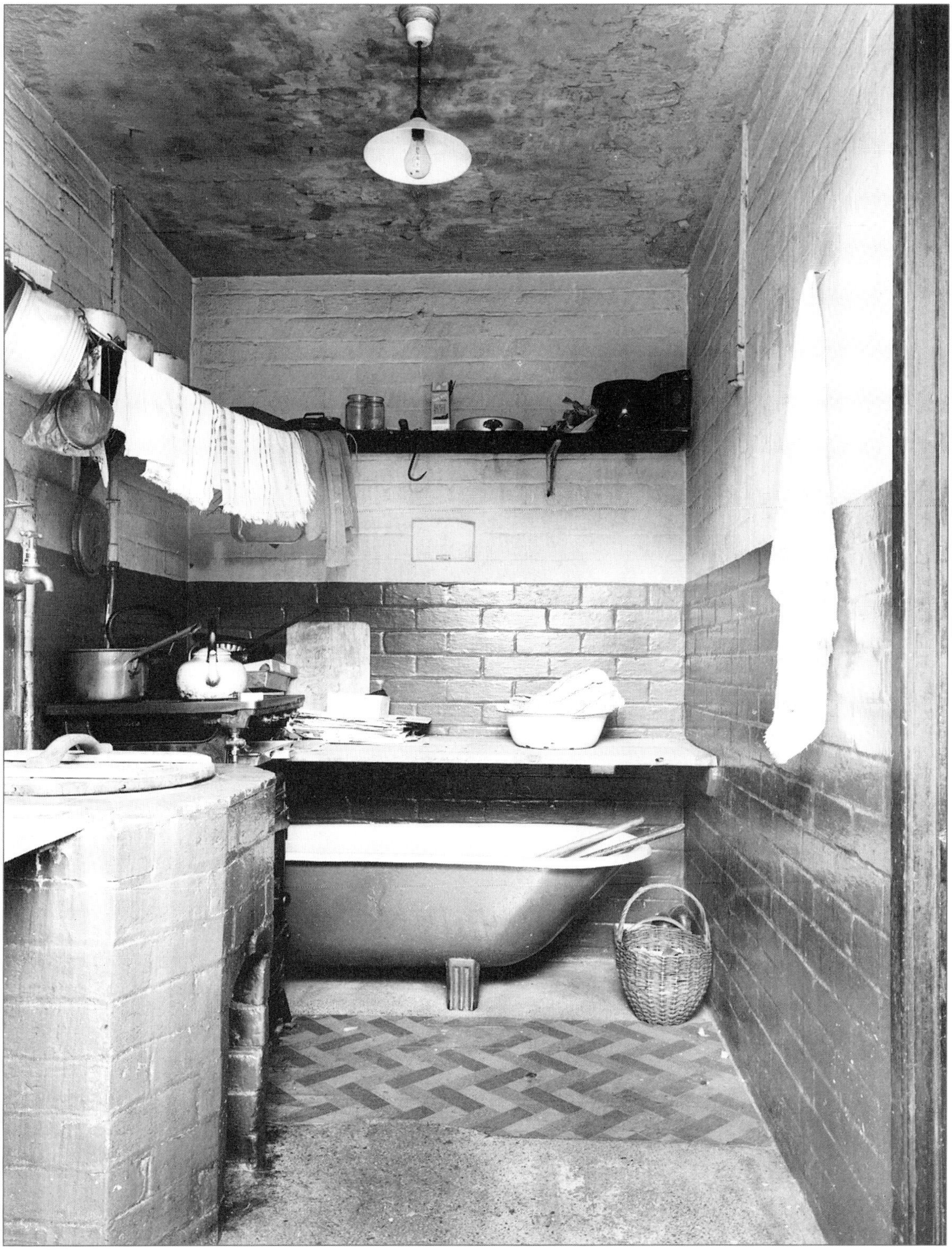

Kitchen on the Penpole Housing Estate, Shirehampton, mid-1950s. This estate had been completed at the end of the First World War, originally to house munitions workers from Avonmouth. This view, taken shortly before modernisation, shows the basic facilities of the original design with a bath, gas cooker, wash copper and sink squeezed into a small room of bare brick less than 6 ft wide.

The residents of a new council flat at Barton House, Barton Hill, show their new home to guests at the official opening, *c.* 1956. Barton Hill was developed in accordance with the 'neighbourhood unit' principle which was fashionable among planners at the end of the Second World War. Fom the mid-1950s blocks of flats, some fifteen storeys high, were built among pockets of Victorian housing retained to preserve the sense of community. The Council's Housing Committee was clearly very proud of them: formal ceremonies attended by the Lord Mayor and other official guests – who would visit some of the tenants – usually marked the opening of the individual blocks.

Shops at Four Acres, Withywood, *c.* 1956. A subsidiary shopping centre built on the Withywood estate developed on the southern edge of Bristol in the 1950s.

Spencer and Norton House in Redcliff. The Redcliff Estate was conceived as one of the City Council's post-war neighbourhood units in the older part of the city. In the 1950s several picturesque streets of small brick Georgian terraced houses in Recliff between Redcliffe Way and the New Cut were obliterated for a mixed development of blocks containing maisonettes, flats and bedsits. The Redcliff development survives in 1999 as probably the most intact example of 1950s City Council planning.

A Weights & Measures inspector checks the actual weight of a sack of coal on a delivery lorry using standard, calibrated scales. The verification of weights and measures was the work of the City Council's Weights & Measures Department, which also carried out spot checks in the street to ensure that goods such as milk, bread and coal were being sold at the correct weight or measurement.

Fire tender at the Bridewell fire station, *c.* 1947. The fire service remained under the control of the Chief Constable until 1948 when it became a separate organisation under the direct control of the City Council.

Redhouse Primary School, Heggard Close, Withywood, *c.* 1956. The building of new schools was second only to the provision of new homes in the immediate post-war period. Between 1945 and 1951, fourteen new schools were built and on 26 October 1956 Redhouse Primary School, designed to accommodate 280 infant and junior schoolchildren was one of twenty-one new schools opened formally in Bristol by Sir David Eccles. By 1973 ninety-one new schools had opened since 1945.

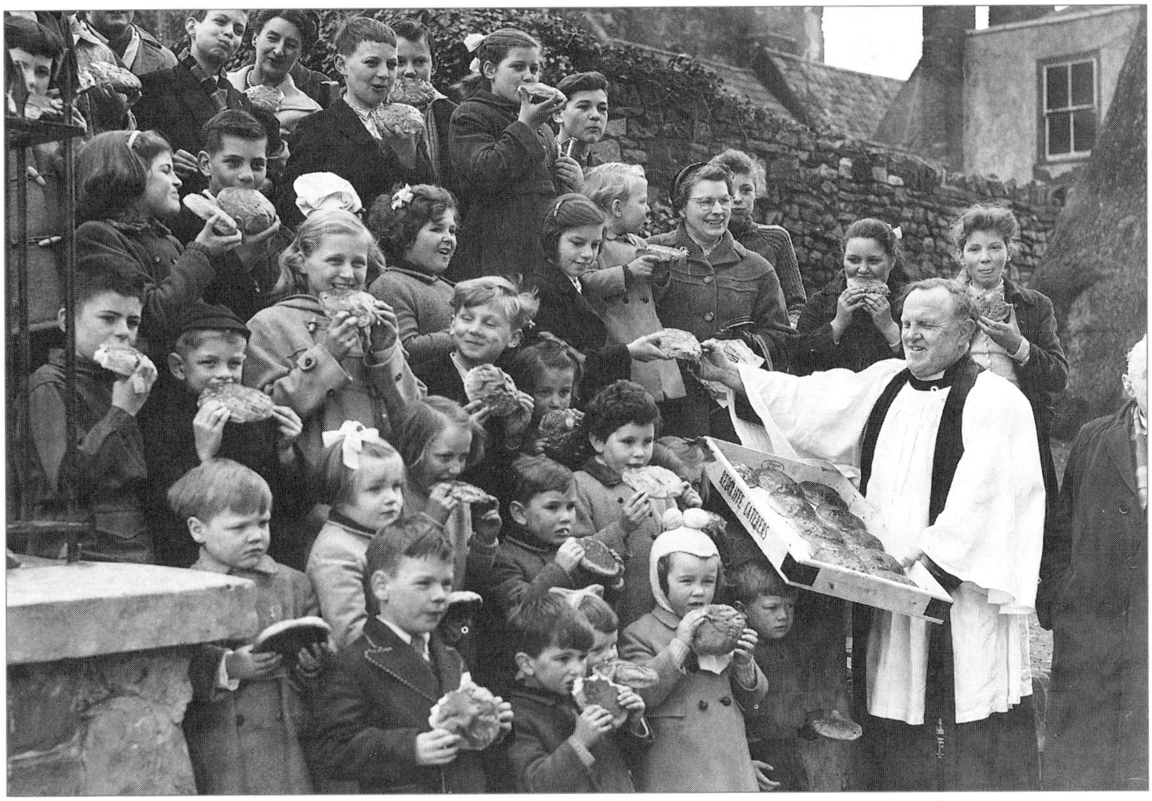

Twopenny starvers, St Michael's Church, Kingsdown, 8 April 1958. This old custom is celebrated every Easter Tuesday when white bread is distributed to poor children in the parish. Here, the Revd F.C. Vyvyan Jones hands out buns to a group of children.

Dr G. Thalben Ball performs on the new Colston Hall organ during the inaugural concert of the new organ, 18 January 1956. Having survived the Blitz, the Colston Hall was damaged by a disastrous fire in 1945 and following an extensive refurbishment reopened in 1951.

Lionel Hampton (left) the well-known American jazz musician performing at the Colston Hall in 1956.

Ella Fitzgerald photographed in Marcos Restaurant after her concert in the Colston Hall on 24 February 1955. The Oscar Peterson Trio was also billed that night.

Mel Torme (1925–99) performing at the Bristol Hippodrome in about 1956. Known as the 'Velvet Frog', Mel Torme often brought his show to an end with a 'tour de force' solo on the drums.

Modern jazz at the Civic Restaurant, College Green, Bristol, 1955. Left to right, Tubby Hayes on tenor saxophone, Derek Humble on alto saxophone and Jimmy Deuchar on trumpet. Just visible at the back are Eddie Taylor on drums, Stan Wasser on bass and Eddie Thompson on piano.

Giant Goram, Blaise Castle Estate, late 1950s. This fair was a regular annual event on the Blaise Castle Estate in the post-war period when 'holidays at home' were popular. It took its name from the legendary giant associated with the estate; several natural features in the limestone landscape on the estate are named after him.

Goram's Fair, Blaise Castle Estate, late 1950s. A clown juggles to an appreciative audience at Goram's Fair in about 1958. Blaise Castle House, which had opened as a Folk Museum in May 1949, can be seen in the background.

Bristol Bulldogs speedway racing on the cinder track at Knowle Stadium, 30 July 1954. This stadium, also a popular venue for greyhound racing, was subsequently built over.

Bristol Zoo, *c.* 1950. Founded in 1835, the zoo had improved its collections from the late 1920s and has since maintained its position as one of the city's chief tourist attractions.

The Queen talking with the Vice-Chancellor of Bristol University, Sir Philip Morris and the Lord Mayor of Bristol, P.W. Raymond at the opening of the new £1 million Engineering School, 5 December 1958; press photographs and television images were then in black and white so it was essential that the press release included the colour of the Queen's outfit – here her coat is described as being a pale lime green.

The 1960s and '70s

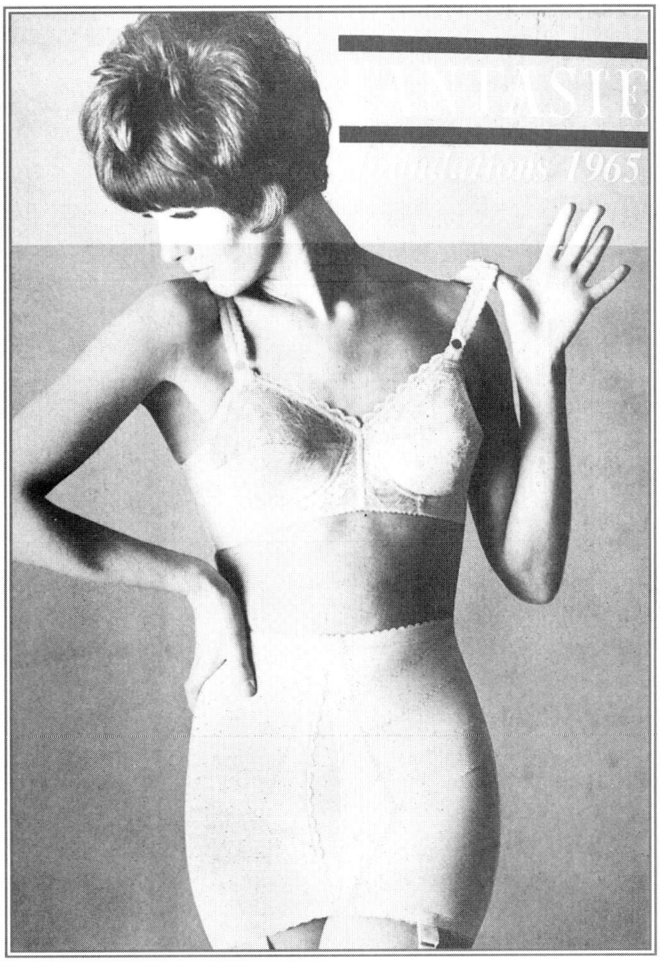

Fantasie Foundations by Unity Corsets, Waters Road, Kingswood, 1965. At the beginning of the century, the clothing and footwear industries were major employers in the city; by the mid-twentieth century they had lost their pre-eminence but G.B. Britain with Tuf shoes and Unity Corsets producing the Fantasie brand demonstrated an ability to respond to changes in the market. But it was the aerospace industry at Filton which continued to be the largest single employer in the city: no longer the Bristol Aeroplane company but a part of the British Aircraft Company and subsequently British Aerospace. Filton's production of Concorde in association with the French brought considerable prestige to the city. A year after Concorde's maiden flight from Filton the SS *Great Britain* was brought home, reflecting a growing appreciation of the city's heritage and the growing importance of the conservation lobby.

The Lord Mayor, Councillor W.G. Cozens, leaving the Lord Mayor's Chapel after the Lord Mayor's Day Service led by the City Sword Bearer, J.L. Purchase. Baker Baker & Co., the Bristol-owned department store, had moved to College Green after its Wine Street premises were destroyed in the Blitz. W.G. Couzins was Lord Mayor from 1959 to 1960.

The City Trumpeters sound a fanfare as a civic procession staged for filming moves off from the quadrangle of Clifton College in August 1963. The number of civic occasions accompanied by formal ceremony dropped in the late twentieth century but in 1999 City Trumpeters were still employed at three church services: Palm Sunday, Rush Sunday and Legal Sunday in October.

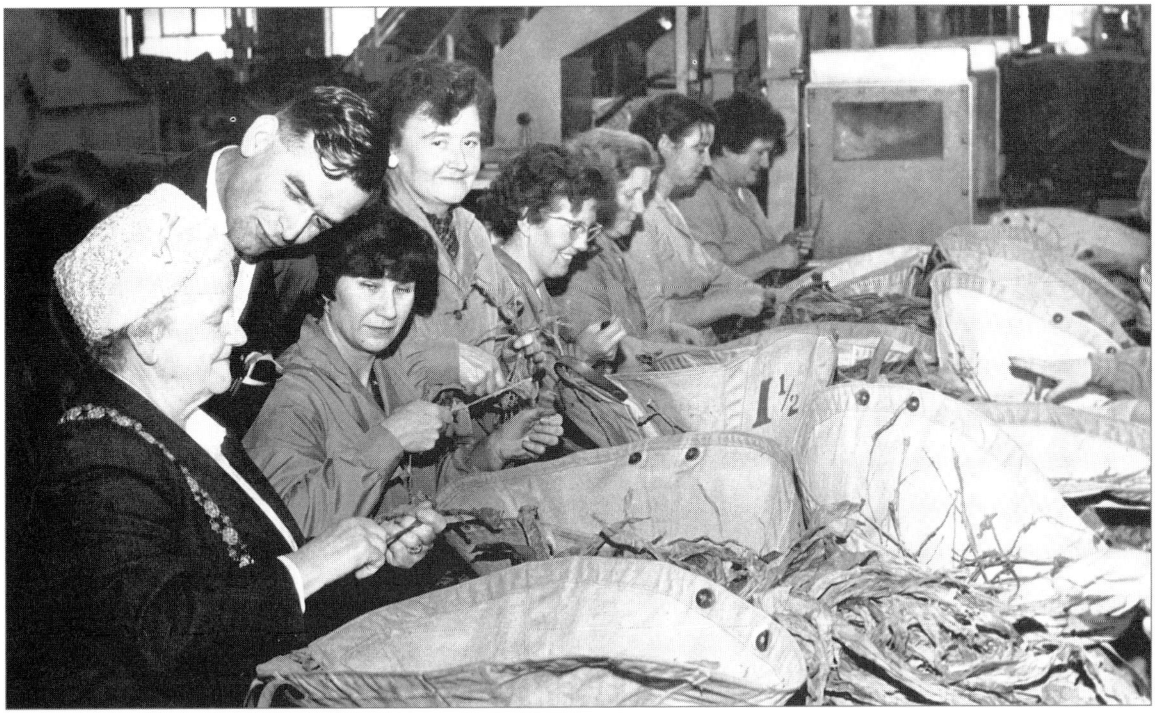

The Lord Mayor, Florence Brown, returns to her old job for a few minutes: stemming tobacco leaf at Wills' Number 1 factory, June 1963. Florence Brown was the first female Lord Mayor of Bristol.

G.B. Britten & Sons Ltd., Kingswood, mid-1960s. Pieces of leather which will eventually form the uppers of boots and shoes are being cut out on a 'clicking' machine.

Redcliff Hill, April 1960. The 1960s witnessed the large-scale demolition of old properties across Bristol to clear the way for the council's ambitious road schemes: this was a time when the supremacy of the motor car was unchallenged and nothing – not even Watts' famous shot tower on Redcliff Hill – was deemed important enough to stand in the way. At the end of the decade most old property on both sides of this road – a fascinating mixture of seventeenth-century timber-framed buildings, Georgian façades and florid Victorian brickwork – was swept away to create a dual carriageway.

Thirteen arches viaduct, Stapleton Road, 1968. The houses on the junction between Muller Road and Stapleton Road were demolished in January 1968 and the thirteen-arch railway viaduct was destroyed in a spectacular controlled explosion in May. The bus emerging from the under the viaduct is a Lodekka bus – a low height double-decker which was produced by Bristol Commercial Vehicles in large numbers for the Bristol Omnibus Company, Crosville and other nationalised bus companies in the Tilling Group during the 1950s and 1960s.

St Andrew's-the-Less, Hotwells Road, *c.* 1960. St Andrew's-the-Less, built in 1872, was demolished in January 1963; further clearances on the corner of Merchants Road and Hotwells Road followed in February and June in preparation for the construction of the new road system over the Cumberland Basin.

A press party being shown the new Plimsoll Bridge over the Cumberland Basin during construction in 1964. Work on the Cumberland Basin Bridge scheme began on 4 February 1963 and it was officially opened by Tom Fraser MP, the Minister of Transport, on 14 April 1965. It was the first scheme in the city designed to assist traffic flow using carriageways at different levels, and the first to be lit with lamps of Swedish design on pillars 85 ft high.

Stapleton Road, Easton, 1960s. Stapleton Road was developed from the 1850s as Bristol's industrial suburbs expanded eastwards. These were demolished to make way for a section of the outer circuit road planned in the 1960s but never completed. The scheme was finally abandoned in 1977 but not before the large-scale demolition of houses in Totterdown and Easton.

Bishop Street, St Pauls, *c.* 1960. Bishop Street was first laid out out with a single row of large late Georgian town houses east of Portland Square around 1800 and these can be seen in the background below the tower of St Paul's Church. The road was extended eastwards as Albert Street contained smaller terraced houses built between 1868 and 1876. It was later renamed as part of Bishop Street but has since disappeared under a new housing development.

Bridge Street, Barton Hill, c. 1960. Barton Hill had developed as a densely populated area of nineteenth century terraced housing with negligible public or private space. Many of the houses were like these seen here in Bridge Street where some forty houses were built between *c.* 1872 and 1876; similar houses were built in Bristol's other industrial suburbs – in Easton, St Philip's Marsh and Bedminster between *c.* 1850 and the late 1870s. They presented an austere front to the street: there are no front gardens, no bay windows and even the shallow roof with a central valley was hidden behind a parapet extension to the front wall. Many of these houses were cleared in the 1950s and 1960s and by the 1990s few survived in anything like their original form. The gas holder in the background was located in Day's Road.

Castlegate House, Brislington, mid-1960s. The building of high-rise blocks of flats by the council began in the mid-1950s and continued for another ten years. Castlegate House was completed in 1964.

Admiring the view – of other blocks of flats – in Kingsdown, *c.* 1967. By the mid-1960s doubts were being raised about the quality of life within a high-rise block but this publicity photograph was originally captioned, 'The upper flats command magnificent views over the city'. If they tired of the view, the residents could always switch on their television set, which by 1963 was found in 82 per cent of British homes.

Right: Council houses, West Town Grove, Brislington. These were 'C' type houses built to the high standards of the Parker Morris Report, *Homes For Today & Tomorrow*, 1961. This report promoted the idea of more flexible internal planning to reflect the greater informality of home life: inside it was recommended that houses should have more space, as people had more possessions, and should be heated throughout. Large picture windows letting in more light were favoured, chimneys all but disappeared and garages became increasingly standard.

Left: Ashton Road, Ashton, 11 July 1968. This was the scene in the low-lying area of Ashton and Bedminster after more than 4 inches of rain fell on almost the whole of Bristol on the night of 10 July 1968; in some roads the water rose to bedroom level.

Right: A pair of houses built privately by George Wimpey & Son in Stockwood. The firm built similar houses in the 1960s in Henbury and Whitchurch; many had dormer windows and weatherboarding, which were fashionable in the 1960s.

Above: Broadmead, summer 1973. Broadmead was designed by the City Council as a replacement for the pre-war shopping centre in Wine Street and Castle Street (see page 34) and was built in stages between the early 1950s and 1960. This part of Broadmead was turned into a pedestrian zone in November 1973.

The inner ring road at Old Market, May 1972. The Tower Hill/Old Market area was designated for office development and car parks in the late 1960s. The result, in the words of Professor John Punter, was 'an unpleasant, unsafe and confusing environment'. The Bristol United Press building is under construction on Temple Way.

Opposite, bottom: The New Entertainment Centre, Frogmore Street, *c.* 1966. Work began on the site in October 1963 and the cinema seating 806 was opened in November 1966 with a showing of *Dr Zhivago*. The complex lasted only a little over 30 years, however, and in 1999 the site was being redeveloped.

In 1961 the somewhat truncated remains of the original Robinson building on the corner of Victoria Street and Redcliff Street were demolished and in April that year this architect's drawing of its replacement were released. Designed by the Robinson group's own in-house company of architects, Group Architects DRG, the new building was a 200-ft high block of fifteen stories. It was Bristol's first high rise block and caused quite a controversy when it was completed in 1963. While the building has been praised for the quality of the intrinsic design and for the success of its siting – occupying a commanding location close to Bristol Bridge – others condemned it as one of the ugliest buildings in Britain! It marked the start of a boom in speculative office development across the city, fuelled by the 22 per cent growth in the service sector in Bristol in the 1960s. Within a ten year period slab and tower office blocks – from Clifton Heights on the Triangle, Clifton to Mercury House in Temple Way radically changed the face of the centre.

The fourteenth-century spire of St John's Church is dwarfed by the twelve-storey St Lawrence House built in 1967 and designed by Alec French & Partners, who were also responsible for the Bristol & West tower overlooking the centre. The intrusion of these drab, dreary blocks of concrete and glass completely transformed the city centre skyline within a relatively short period and took place to a background of mounting criticism.

The Lord Mayor, Florence Brown, with the Sheriff's wife, Mrs Ainslie Baker, at Oldbury Court Youth Club meets (left to right) Tony Bird, Chris Alderman, Phil Taylor and Brian Coombs, November 1963. Florence Brown was the first female Lord Mayor of Bristol.

Mrs L. Coles, a resident of Hills Almshouses, Jacobs Wells Road is presented with a Christmas parcel by the Lord Mayor, Florence Brown in December 1963. The almshouses were founded by T.W. Hill of Clifton in 1867 for twelve old and deserving women. Witnessing the occasion are Miss A.G. Hicks (centre) and Miss E. Mitchell (right), who look as if they have seen it all before.

Regent Street, Clifton, 3 September 1966. In the 1960s Clifton Village wore a somewhat dilapidated air – as these rather tatty shop fronts attest – but who is that crossing the road? It is none other than Cary Grant, a leading Hollywood star, who was born Archie Leach in relatively humble circumstances in Fishponds in 1904. Here, aged sixty-two, he is seen crossing the road with his twenty-eight-year-old wife, Diane Canon, with their six-month-old daughter, Jennifer, in the pram. Cary Grant was in Bristol to see his eighty-nine-year-old mother.

Cary Grant and Diane Canon crossing the corner of Royal York Crescent and Regent Street with the Trustee Savings Bank in the background. It subsequently became a hat shop. Beyond the bank is a bomb site which was later filled. The photographer was Dennis Williams, who worked for the *Evening Post*.

Bristol Airport, *c.* 1965. The airport at Lulsgate, originally built for military purposes during the Second World War, replaced Whitchurch Airport in 1958. Here the control tower is seen framed by two aircraft – one a Cambrian Airways Vickers Viscount (G-AMOH). The council had established an airport committee in 1929 and the running of the airport remained in the City's hands until 1996.

Narrow Quay, *c.* 1963. A Royal Navy minesweeper is berthed beside a venerable looking crane on the quayside – a reminder that in the 1960s this was still a working dock. Mixed cargoes, including wines from France, continued to be unloaded on the quay opposite until the end of the decade. Then, within just a few years, in the early 1970s the commercial vessels finally left the City Docks, the cranes were taken down and a working activity that had continued in an unbroken line since the mid-thirteenth century when these quays were built had gone.

Concorde 002, the British prototype, takes off from Filton on 9 April 1969 on its inaugural flight, watched by a large crowd; the French prototype had made its first flight a month earlier on 2 March. Ten of the twenty production Concordes were assembled at Filton, the other ten at Toulouse: the production model was distinguished by a longer fuselage and slightly different tail fin design. Concorde 002 is now preserved at Yeovilton.

The following year saw another major Bristol engineering achievement attracting national media attention when Brunel's great iron steamship, the SS *Great Britain* of 1843, was towed back to her original dry dock following a long exile beached at Sparrow Cove on the Falkland Islands. At first the City Council was less than enthusiastic about her resting place as it intended filling in this part of the Floating Harbour to make way for part of a planned outer circuit road! The road scheme was eventually abandoned and the City reconciled to the ship, which was soon established as one of Bristol's major tourist attractions. The SS *Great Britain* is seen here entering the Cumberland Basin, 5 July 1970.

Water Festival, St Augustine's Reach, 1973. The closure of the City Docks after 1970 transformed the working dock into a large tract of derelict land close to the heart of the city and presented the City Council with a major problem of regeneration. The original parliamentary closure bill of 1969 had included the filling in of a large part of the Floating Harbour for commercial use in line with the strict zoning of functions which had governed planning philosophy since the 1940s. But the return of the SS *Great Britain*, the series of water festivals and power boat races staged from the early 1970s drew public attention to the amenity value of the docks: plans were changed to incorporate a diversity of uses including light industry, museums, shops and homes.

Lord Beswick, chairman of British Aerospace and the Lord Mayor, Ted Wright, sit on a Shand Mason horse-drawn fire engine of *c.* 1906 at the opening of the Bristol Industrial Museum in M Shed on Princes Wharf, 7 April 1978.

Modern Bristol

Late twentieth century expansion of greater Bristol continued, albeit largely outside the city boundaries in South Gloucestershire. Closer to the centre, regeneration and conservation dominated City planning, working in partnership with a variety of other organisations. In 1999, large-scale redevelopment of the City Docks and the centre was under way. Some of the surviving nineteenth century commercial buildings in Victoria Street were restored but not this façade of polychrome brick arches, which came down in early September 1997.

Ivor Aitken's shoe repair shop, Cotham Hill, July 1986. Ivor Aitken and his wife are photographed shortly before the closure of this family business established in 1919 in Abbotsford Road, Cotham. Many small family-run shops which were a vital part of the local community closed in the latter part of the century, succumbing to the pressure from chain stores and out-of-town shopping centres. In the late twentieth century the majority of people travelled further to do their shopping than at the beginning of the century.

Stapleton Road, Easton, August 1992. The Easton Renewal Area was set up by the City Council in January 1991 to revive the area by improving homes and revitalising the local economy.

Clifton Down Shopping Centre, Whiteladies Road, May 1982.

Galleries Shopping Centre, Union Street, *c.* 1991. The Galleries Shopping Centre was developed on the site of Fairfax House, an early 1960s block, and completed in 1991.

The Bristol International Balloon Fiesta, 1980s. In the late twentieth century Bristol became closely associated with hot air ballooning and has even been described as the 'balloon capital of the world'. Don Cameron started the manufacture of balloons in Bristol in 1970 and the first balloon festival was staged in 1979; since then this annual event has become established as the most important of its kind in Europe.

St Paul's Festival, 1991. The first St Paul's Carnival was held in 1968 and has since become one of the city's major annual events.

Tom Jones at the Colston Hall, December 1994. The City Council-run hall continues to offer a wide range of entertainment from classical concerts to popular entertainment. Photographs of Tom Jones on stage are often blurred around the hips: this is, indeed, a rare view of the Welsh singer standing almost still.

Molly Coghill, a museum volunteer, demonstrating butter making in the thatched dairy behind Blaise Castle House Museum in 1987. The dairy was designed by John Nash and built in about 1804 for John Harford, owner of the Blaise Castle Estate. It continued to serve as a working dairy for the estate until about 1920 and when the museum opened in May 1949 the dairy was opened as a static exhibit. Badly damaged by fire on 13 June 1984, the dairy was subsequently restored and from 1986 butter making demonstrations became a regular feature of events organised by museum staff under the watchful eye of Mrs Coghill, a qualified dairy technologist.

Wine Festival, Exhibition Centre, City Docks, 1982. Disused transit sheds on St Augustine's Reach were given a new lease of life in the 1970s: E shed nearest the centre with its attractive frontage of 1894 designed by the Bristol architect Edward Gabriel became Watershed, a complex of shopping, the Bristol Arts Centre and Radio West. The two sheds beyond – U and V sheds – were converted into a major exhibition centre by the City Council and private enterprise and were used to host exhibitions and trade fairs including the internationally renowned World Wine Fair.

The *Sand Sapphire* (left) and the *Sand Diamond* at Hotwell Dock, September 1987. These ships – along with the *Harry Brown* – brought in sand dredged from the Bristol Channel and kept alive a little of the atmosphere of the working City Docks after most other ships had left; but they relocated to Avonmouth in 1989 and within ten years new houses covered their former berth.

Portbury, an 0–6–0 saddle tank locomotive formerly owned by the Port of Bristol tentatively negotiates overgrown track in Ashton Meadows on the former Great Western Railway branch from Ashton Junction to the City Docks on 19 November 1995. *Portbury* was built in 1917 by the Avonside Engine Co., Ltd, Filwood Road, Fishponds, and spent most of her life working at the Port's sidings at Avonmouth. Made redundant by dieselisation in the 1950s, *Portbury* survived scrapping and in 1988 was returned to working order at the Bristol Industrial Museum. *Portbury* is operated by the museum's volunteers on a summer week-end service along the quayside with another ex-Port Authority locomotive, *Henbury*, built by Pecketts of Bristol in 1937. In 1995, operations were extended about one and a half miles up the branch towards Ashton Junction. This length of track was last used in May 1987 and by the early 1990s was rapidly disappearing under brambles, buddleia and ivy. The line was returned to working order, however, by the railway's small team of volunteers in time for the operation of a three-coach steam shuttle during the Festival of the Sea in May 1996. The following year *Portbury* was withdrawn for a major overhaul and is due to reappear in service in 2000 painted in the original grey livery in which it was delivered, replacing the blue it has carried since 1988.

The Tobacco Bonds at Canons Marsh on the clear sunny morning of Sunday 29 May 1988 at about 7.00 a.m., just moments before being demolished with high explosives.

Moments after the detonation a huge cloud of dust rises, obscuring the debris and covering the large crowd of spectators on Princes Bridge.

And once the dust cloud had dispersed, the warehouses had gone and a new view opened up. Work began shortly afterwards on the construction of the new national headquarters of Lloyds Bank.

Lloyds Bank Headquarters, 1993. This stone faced curved building, designed by Arup Associates, replaced the warehouses. After lowering the quay walls, the amphitheatre in front of the building was laid out for public use in 1990.

Baltic Wharf Housing, July 1986. The first waterside housing development at Rownham Mead was completed in about 1980 and was followed in 1985 by the building of 272 homes across the dock on derelict land, used as timber yards until the 1970s. Although named 'Baltic' Wharf this second development is located a short distance to the east of Baltic Wharf and actually occupies former timber wharfs – Onega, Canada, Cumberland and Gefle, or Garle in Sweden, laid out in the nineteenth century.

Crest Apartments, Cumberland Road, 1999. Overlooking Whapping Wharf and the sidings of the Bristol Harbour Railway are these dockside homes built for Crest Homes and completed in December 1998. They were designed by John Bignell of the Architecture & Planning Group based in Gas Ferry Road. While these homes form an attractive block, plans for further developments of large blocks of apartments on sites closer to the quayside have encountered strong local opposition from people concerned about the loss of the working character of the docks.

Church Road, Westbury-on-Trym, 18 October 1990. A few older properties somehow managed to survive most of the twentieth century without seemingly being touched by it: houses which in terms of their technology and furnishings were still rooted in the late nineteenth century – the media call them 'time capsules'. One such was no. 23 Church Road (left) which created quite a sensation in the local press when it was put on the market by estate agents Allen & Harris in October 1990. From the outside the house looked no different from its neighbours but inside it was still lit by gas and in the back kitchen a Victorian cooking range, wash copper and stoneware sink survived intact.

Rear of 23 Church Road, Westbury-on-Trym. The back kitchen seen from the garden; the house was subsequently modernised. This was the home of Bill and Edith Pepworth (see page 25). Bill died in 1968 but Edith survived him for twenty-one years and resolutely refused to install electricity.

Stoneware sink on a brick plinth at 23 Church Road, possibly dating from 1871 when the house was altered, and used by Edith Pepworth until her death in November 1989.

Above: Basement kitchen, 50 Granby Hill, 9 May 1989. This house was built in about 1789 and the basement kitchen had long been abandoned. In 1989 it still contained, from left, the original wash copper, a Victorian kitchen range in the fireplace, an iron baking oven and on the extreme right a small iron hot plate for stewing; only a disused Belfast sink propped on its side on the right and the author's notebook resting on it belonged to the twentieth century.

Right: Front parlour, 21 Nottingham Road, Bishopston, 4 May 1995. This house managed to retain most of its original fittings dating from about 1891 until the spring of 1995 when the elderly occupant decided to modernise it and install electricity – some sixty years or more after it was laid in the road outside! The furnishings and paintwork in the front parlour had scarcely changed since the early part of the century: two gaslamps on decorative brackets on the chimney breast were still in use.

City centre, 1985. By the late 1970s the row of old buildings fronting the centre on St Augustine's Parade (see page 20), a mixture of medieval, Georgian and Victorian buildings, were in a poor state but in 1982 a sensitive restoration scheme was started, which acknowledged the considerable sentimental value of these buildings to Bristolians. The decision was made to remove the fake half-timbering added to the buildings formerly occupied by the tramway company . . .

. . . but the tramways clock was returned to the restored buildings in 1985. Will it still be there in 2100?

Acknowledgements and Picture Credits

This book would not have been possible without the support of many people who gave me their time and lent me their precious original photographs for inclusion in the book. In particular I would like to thank John Williams and Richard Burley and their colleagues at the Bristol Record Office who not only made available many of the photographs reproduced here but also helped answer my many enquiries. I also received invaluable assistance from Sir George White, Mike Hooper, Roy Vaughan and Denis Willams. I would also like to thank John Bignell of the Architecture and Planning Group, Anne Bradley, Archivist, John Bryant of Bristol & Region Archaeological Service, Kieran Costello, Peter Davey, Oliver Dearden, Dawn Dyer at the Central Reference Library, Paul Elkin, Tracy Guiry, @ Bristol, Tony Hall, Peter Heydon, Robert Huddlestone, Mike Jenner, Alison Jones, Archivist, Andy King, Curator of Industrial and Maritime History, Bristol Museums Service, David Martin, Manager of the Bristol Harbour Railway, David Mellor of the Alec French Partnership, Paul Preager, Concert Planning Manager at the Colston Hall, Mike Tozer, David Williams, Archive Assistant and Chris Young of the SS Great Britain Trust.

All the photographs are from the Bristol Record Office and the Central Reference Library except the following:
Sir George White: 2, 29, 30, 31, 32, 33, 54 (bottom), 66, 67, 71, 74 (top), 75, 76
Roy Vaughan: 28 (middle and bottom), 36 (bottom), 37 (bottom), 38 (top), 40, 41 (middle and bottom), 42, 65, 68 (top)
Bristol City Museum & Art Gallery: 26–7, 113
Mike Hooper: 32, 63, 64, 82 (bottom), 83, 94 (top), 95 (top), 96, 97, 98 (top)
Planning, Transport & Development, Bristol City Council: 110 (bottom), 111 (top), 112 (bottom), 114 (top), 117 (top and middle), 120
Denis Williams: 72, 86 (bottom), 87, 89 (top), 94 (bottom)
Peter Davey: 21, 39, 70
Peter Heydon: 111 (bottom), 112 (top), 116
The Bristol Aerospace Collection: 107 (top)
David J. Fowler: 115
Paul Elkin: 108 (bottom)
Judith Angerson: 23 (bottom)
The Colston Hall: 113 (top)
Tom Hignell: 25 (bottom)
The SS Great Britain Trust: 107 (bottom)
Mahala Menzies: 57 (bottom)
The Architecture & Planning Group: 117 (bottom)
Hayes Davidson: Back endpaper.